JOHN HART

AN ORTHOGRAPHIE
1569

A Scolar Press Facsimile

THE SCOLAR PRESS LIMITED
MENSTON, ENGLAND
1969

THE SCOLAR PRESS LIMITED
20 Main Street, Menston, Yorkshire, England

Printed in Great Britain by
The Scolar Press Limited
Menston, Yorkshire, England

NOTE

Reproduced (original size) from a copy in the possession of the Editor.

The importance of John Hart's *Orthographie* in the history of English linguistics has long been recognized, and is evident from the importance attached to his work by historians of English pronunciation in the sixteenth-century. The text has been elaborately edited in two volumes (biography, bibliographical apparatus, text and phonology) by Professor Bror Danielsson (Stockholm, 1955-63), and E. J. Dobson's *English Pronunciation 1500-1700* provides a thorough phonology (I, 62-88). The copy here reproduced (not recorded in Danielsson's census) conforms mainly to Danielsson's group G4. Additions and comments in manuscript by a subsequent owner are probably *ca.* 1650.

References: STC 12890; Alston, VI, 519.

Margiliss.

AN ORTHO-

graphie,

conteyning the due
order and reason, howe to
write or paint thimage of mannes
voice, most like to the life or
nature. Composed by
I. H. Chester
Heralt.

The contents wherof are
next folowing.

Sat cito, si at bene.
Sat cito si sat bene.

Anno. 1569.

¶ The Table of the Contents.

Iacobus Coogenes Bredanus, Lectori.

ANglia cum lachrimis ducens suspiria corde,
   Lucida replebat talibus astra sonis:
Heu me, cur Græcis, Hæbræis atq́; Latinis,
   Verba typis aptis explicuisse datur?
Et generosa tamen nunquã gens Anglica rectis
   Quæ loquitur potuit pingere verba notis?
Talia conquestam diuam Chesterus heraldus
   Audijt: hinc patriæ suppetiasq́; parat.
Atq́; dolens tristem casum conatibus instat
   Dedecoris tantas obliterare notas.
Ac literas multas, quas confinxère parentes
   Sustulit, his etenim debitus vsus abest.
Inde nouos secum, quo possit commodus esse
   Omnibus, effinxit composuitq́; typos.
Non hic sufficiunt quos olim prisca vetustas
   Excogitàre typos, maius at vrget opus.
Sunt literæ hîc quarum virtutes atq́; valores
   In alijs linguis non reperire queas.
Quare certatim grates quibus Anglica cordi,
   Authori & scriptis reddite quisq́; suis.

¶. I.   The

The compositor to
the Reader.

YOu may be incouraged by mée,
  Untill you haue red all this booke,
Loth I was the workman to bée,
  Which yet at length in hand I tooke,
And truly as I found and kno,
  In paffing through the doubtfull way,
The drift and reafon tooke me fo,
  That when I fhould the olde affay,
Mine often miffing did bewray,
  That my fenfes were wholy bent,
To vfe and kéepe the new intent.

¶ To the doubtfull of the
English Orthographie, Iohn
Hart Chester heralt wisheth
all health and pros-
peritie.

RTHOGRA-
phie is a Greeke
woorde signifying
true writing, which
is when it is framed
with reasō to make
vs certayne wyth
what letters euery
member of our speach ought to bee
written. By which definition wee
ought to vse an order in writing,
which nothing cared for vnto this
day, our predecessors and we haue ben
(as it were) drouned in a maner of negligence, to bee contented with such
maner of writing as they and we now,
haue found from age to age. Without
any regard vnto the seuerall parts of
the voice, which the writing ought
to represent. And so haue written at
a ven-

Orthographia:
recte scribendi
ars.

Ordo, ratio, certa.

Literæ sunt notæ
particularæ vocis.

a venture, without thorder and reason, which is in euerie perfect writing:
wherein there ought to be a meane, as
in euery thing elfe, according to thefe
verfes.

Est modus in rebus, funt certi deniq̃, fines,

  Quos vltra citraq̃, nequit confiftere rectum.

And though in this treatife the perfection of the fubiect be not attayned
vnto, yet is there an entrance giuen,
wherby it may be the eafilier finifhed
by fome others herafter, whofe better
learning and experience may caufe
them to worke more fubftantiallye
then is herein done, according to the
faying of Quintilian in the laft chapter of his twelvth booke, *De inftitutio-
ne oratoria,* where he encourageth men
to that ftudie which mought make
them perfect in life and doctrine : being a farre greater matter thā perfectly to write : which is therefore much
the eafier to be taken in hand, attayned vnto, and vfed, where he fayth :
*Natura enim nos ad mentem optimam genuit,
adeoq̃, difcere meliora volentibus promptum eft,*

                                        vt

The Epistle

vt verè intuenti mirum sit illud magis, malos esse tam multos. Which signifieth, truly Nature hath begotten vs to the best minde, and it is so readie for the willing to learne the best things, that he that would consider it well, shoulde maruayle the more, there should be so manye euill men. And I touching writers, doe maruaile our predcecessours haue continued in the disorder and confusion which is in our English writing. And a little after he sayeth, *Omnia breuiora reddet ordo & ratio & modus*, which signifieth order and reason and meane, doe make all things more briefe and easie. And further, *Sed culpa est in præceptoribus prima*, and so he continueth to this sense: but the first fault is in the schoolemaisters, which kepe childer willingly, partly by couetousnesse to get therby their longer small hires, partly by ambition that the thing they promise shuld be thought the harder to be lerned, partly also by ignorance or negligence in teaching: and secondly in vs, bicause we think

it

it better to continue in that we know,
than to learne the thing wee knowe
not. Wherfore though none of them
hath confidered thabufe of our writing, and indeuored the beft they
could to feeke the correction therof,
yet me thinke they fhould not be offended with him that fhall doe his
good will therein. Which I haue done
as hereafter with the due confiderati-
on what letters ar, and thereafter framed their vfe to be knowen certainly
for the members of our fpeech. Wherin is kept the meane according to the
abouefayd two verfes neyther to bee
troubled with exceffe, nor to be in pe-
nurie for want. To the vnderftanding
wherof the readieft waye is to begin,
and fo to folow in order: and not pre-
pofteroufly to begin at the latter ende
where fome may take occafion to bee
offended (at the fight of the ftraunge
letters) if they fhould not confider the
reafons alledged, with the inftructi-
ons hereafter, to prepare them toward
the reading thereof. For who fo is fo
greedy

The Epistle

greedy to ride, that when he seeth a
sadled horse, he will needes leape on,
he may sooner repent him than haue
his desire. Therfore, before you builde
be sure of a good foundation, and
then you may worke certainly and
not by chaunce. And accordinglye
here foloweth a certain order of true
writing of the speech, founded vpon
Reason mother of all sciences: wherwith you may happily be profi-
ted, and so health and the
grace of God be with
you. So be
it.

Faultes escaped in part of the Copies of this first impression.

Folio 3.page.2.line.3.Who so, read, So, who so.

Fol 7.pa.2.li.4. tung, read, writing.

Fol.12.pa.2.lin.23. propable, read, probable.

Fol.29.pa.1.lin 22.23. in this chapter, read, here-after.

Fol.34.pa.1.lin.14. siue, read, sine.

From the.34. to the. 64. leaues, they are wrong numbred. Which are to be corrected ere the table can serue.

Fol.42.pa.1.lin.3, such, much, should be, suG, muG.

Fol.43.pa.1.lin. 22, for, fol.36.make. 40.

Fol. 43.pa.2.lin.1. for, fol.34 35.make.38.39.

Fol. 61.pa.2.lin.15, n, read, m, or n.

Fol.63.pa. 2. lin.22. gh, read, gli.

Fol.66.pa.1,lin. 6. Gar, read, Car.

The Preface, wherein is

brieflye conteyned the reasons, causes, commodities, summe and effect of this Treatise.

An non Bella Troiana ordin.. abscu..

WRITING IS reasonable marking or grauing, or laying on of some colour diffe-ring from the su-perficies or grounde, to signifie ye writers mind to the beholder, which is instructed in that maner. By which definition it ap-peereth that euery ma may deuise his pri-uate maner for himself or such other as he will impart it vnto. Cornelius Tacitus & Diodorus do write that the Egyptians did first vse the figures of the diuerse sub-stance in mannes knowledge, thereby to represent the actes of Princes about their Obeliscos for their posteritie, and their mindes one to thother liuing: which was a tedious way, and therfore are we bound to acknowledge the benefite recepued of the first inuenters of our present maner,

A.ij.   Wher-

Marginalia:

1

Scriptura est pictura vocis humanæ. —

A pictura; illinit colorer diuersos a superficie.

pictura est retentio figuræ, aut per figuram linearem superficialem.

Scriptura res arbitraria.

scriptum ... ut ... Ægypty molis & simulacris res qas Hieroglyphica dicunt; ubi baut

Scriptura per sculpturam facit ad mentem agendis visibilia minus ex pictura nota ut Vrbs, Theatra.

Scriptura & loquela finem conueniunt, nempe ut mentem loquentis & scribentis alteri sensibilem faciant. sc. legenti & audienti. sed modis diuersis finem suum sequuntur.

The Preface

wherby a man may signifie and leaue behinde him for euer whatsoeuer he can speake. And what writer doth nearest and most iustly decerne the diuers voices of the speach, he is best able to describe and paint the same with his pen, which maner of writing (for that it is most commodious) is treated on hereafter, for by the like, things worthie memorie, are defended and preserued from all iniury of forgetfulnesse, whereby is left vnto vs from right auncient times, of our most worthy predecessors, the most holy will of God, and necessary doctrines of many of his elect by diuine inspiration, with many other humaine pollicies and reasonable instructions and counsels written by many wise and studious men, and the same multiplied by their posteritie, which by experience we see are greatly to the increase, noriture, maintenaunce and defence of the few better sort, from the violence of the barbarous multitude. To the vnderstanding wherof, is first necessary the knowledge of letters, and where most of the people doe best know them, there is most

moſt proſperitie and beſt aſſuraunce . To
which ende is this treatiſe, for the profite
of the multitude, and that by opening the
windowe whereby is light giuen to decerne betwixt perfection and barbarous-
neſſe, ſo as euery reaſonable creature v-
niuerſally (of what nation ſoeuer vnder-
ſtanding it) may be a perfite iudge howe
euerye language ought to bee written.
Which is vppon the conſideration of the
ſeuerall voices of the ſpeach, and the vſe
of their ſeuerall markes for them, which
we cal letters. But in the moderne & preſent maner of writing (aſwell of certaine
other languages as of our English) there
is ſuch confuſion and diſorder, as it may
be accounted rather a kinde of ciphring,
or ſuch a darke kinde of writing, as the
beſt and readieſt wit that euer hath bene,
could, or that is or ſhalbe, can or may, by
the only gift of reaſon, attaine to the rea-
dy and perfite reading thereof, without a
long and tedious labour, for that it is vn-
fit and wrong ſhapen for the proportion of
the voice. Whereas the new maner hereafter (thoughe it ſeeme at the firſt very

A.iij.   ſtraunge

Scriptura fit per literas

Scriptura est loquela permanens signata, certa.

Librarum confusio & æquiuocatio, difficultatis causa in discendo.

The Preface

straunge, hard and vnprofitable) by the reading only therof, will proue it selfe fit, easie and delectable, and that for whatsoeuer English may be writté in that order.

Yet I knowe that some at the first opening of the booke, and seeing of the straunge figures and maner of writing, wil say, what shal we now be set to schole againe euen to our A.B.C: then had we liued to long. Here are faire promises, like to this, that the toppes of trees shalbe planted in the grounde, and the rootes spred in the aire, and beare so their fruits, with such other rashe derisions as doe make me laugh when I thinke on them. And so considering the common opinion of mankinde to be so earnestlye giuen to thimitation of their predecessors condicions and maner of doings, and (as it were with tooth and nayle) to maintaine for the best, those wherein they themselues haue bene trayned and vsed from their Cradell, I haue stayed from publishing hereof many yeares. For whosoeuer shal speake or write for thamendment of anye whatsoeuer their customes, he shall be

of

Suu cuiqz pulchru.

The Preface

of the most part frowned at, or at least
his purpose accounted to be superfluous
and nothing necessarie. And will not let
at first to saye, that if anye fault were, it
could not be left to these our dayes vncor=
rected, seeing so manye wise and learned
men in many Ages haue bene before vs,
and therfore it is but folly to lende eye or
eare therebnto. Which notwithstanding
I trust it may doe some good (though not
in my dayes) to the posteritie, for whose
sakes I thinke my labour well bestowed,
for commonlye thinuentions of the li=
uing, are rather enuied than fauored. You
know that euery man is as much bounde
to publish the thing which he hopeth may
profite, as to keepe silence of that he doub=
teth may be hurtfull: & that as transgres=
sors of good & reasonable lawes are wor=
thily punished, so thinuetors of profitable
things, though not rewarded according
to their desertes, yet are they of the most
barbarous people fauored & born withall.
And as no man ought to trauell in this life
onely or chiefly for himselfe and his next
bloud, to the hinderance of others, but for

A.iiij.   the

the common welth of his country, though with daunger of life, or the price thereof in dæde. Who so may profite his country in any condicion, and especiallye wyth small cost and no daunger, he were vnnaturall to be a niggarde thereof: though peraduenture the trauayle, the cost and time which I haue spent in other affaires thereby attaining to the knowledge to be able to compose this worke hath bene more deare vnto me than some wil think. And I right wel know it can none otherwise be allowed, than as the learned sort by Experience (Mistres of al Arts) shall finde it reasonable and profitable : by whose iudgements as well mine aduersaries as I, must of necessity be ruled, when time may serue, and in the meane while I shall be armed with pacience to beare the anger of such as are obstinately bent to maintaine their custome and vse.

In any chaunge which is to be attempted in any peoples maner of doings, there is requisite eyther excelling authoritie, or a good perswasion of a common commoditie. The first must be obeyed what

chaunge

[marginalia: So who so]

[marginalia: Correctio, vel authoritate, vel vtilitate nih'luv]

chaunge of any inferiour purpose soeuer may come therof. And thother is at libertie to be taken or refused, according as experience, maye finde it profitable or hurtfull.

Wherefore I will nowe signifie vnto such as haue not wilfully professed themselues to be obstinate in their custome, that the vse and experience of thorder of this following English Orthographie, shall bring these commodities following. First it shall cause the naturall English knowing no letter, to be able to learne to decerne and easily to reade (whatsoeuer he may see before him so writtten or printed) so soone as he were able to learne readily, and perfectly to know and name, the number of figures or members of the bodie and substance of our voice and speach, & so obseruing the new or straunge order hereafter written, the learned man may instruct any naturall English reasonable creature, to read English, in one quarter of the time that euer any other hath heretofore bene taught to reade, by any former maner. And in what lesse time, and

B.j.   how

Noua ĉmendanda aut ex authoritate — ab experientia vtilitatis

The first commoditie for the vn-learned naturall English people: No more labour to spell then to know the letters.

learne to reade in one quarter of the time.

how much more easie and readie, it will
be for the writer or Printer, Reader and
hearer, I will not write, but leaue it to
the iudgement of the Reader, of the sayd
following treatise, and to the experience
it selfe as occasion shall serue.

Secondly, if anye man of one or other
nation, would gladly learne to pronounce
any straunge speach which is accustomed
to be written so confusedly, as it were (of
necessitie) only to be learned by the liuely
voice, and not able to be red by any order
of their writing, as maye be sayde of the
Welsh and Irish, yet vsing thorder hereafter, he shall be able to write eyther of
them (or any other like) euen as iustly in
the least voice, sound or breath, as it shall
be naturallye spoken vnto him, and so
read it againe perfitely, when and where
soeuer he may see it, though many yeares
thereafter, and though he vnderstode no
worde therof, and that by the reason hereafter shewed . Whereas by our present
disorder it often happeneth that a verye
good iudgement , maye doubt in what
sound, many a word shoulde be pronounced,

Secondly for
straungers
or the rude
countrie
English
man, which
may desire
to read
English as
the best
sort vse to
speake it.

ced, vntill by reason of the sentence it bee
founde, and many a man doth scantlye
know how the writing of his owne name
should be sounded, by which disorders and
confusions, there can be made no perfite
Dictionarie nor Grammer, which are
very commodious for any straunger that
desireth to learne our tongue by Arte, or
for the rude to learne to speake well, as
every childe that hath learned his Latine
Grammer knoweth.

Thirdly, we should not neede to vse a-
boue the two thirdes or three quarters at
most, of the letters which we are nowe
constreyned to vse, and so saue the one
third, or at least the one quarter, of the paper, ynke, and time which we now spend
superfluously in writing and printing.
And last of all, English Latinistes maye
hereby vnderstand, the Italian and high
Dutch and Welshe pronounciation of
their letters, which by presumption is
verie neare as the auncient Greekes and
Latines did, being according to thorder
and reason of their predecessors first inuention of them, whereby our errors are

B.ij.   the

Thirdly,
for cost and
time saued.

saue paper, ynke
& time.

And last,
for a helpe
for the lear-
ned sort
which de-
sire to pro-
nounce
other tongs
aright.

to vnder-
stand
Latine
spoken or
written.

the better perceyued, and in the ende of the booke a certaine example how the Italian, high Duch, French, and Spanyard doe vse to pronounce Latine and their owne languages. Truly the commodities aforesaid (which I perswade my self may follow) and the hinderance and confusion wherein I see we are, doe cause me to put it into light: to thend such as are able to be iudges, may be occasioned to consider therof. Whose like (I meane the learned sort) haue bene in times past, causers of our present maner of writing, by turning their penne to adde or diminish, alter or chaunge, as they thought meete into other letters and Carrects, much differing from the olde Saxon maner. And the liuing doe knowe themselues no further bounde to this our instant maner, than our predecessors were to the Saxon letters and writing, which hath bene altered as the speach hath chaunged, much differing from that which was vsed within these fiue hundreth, I maye say within these two hundreth yeares: which I considered of about .xx. yeares passed, and
thought

thought it worth my labour, if I coulde
finde the meane of remedie, of our present
abuse. And so framed a treatise therevp=
pon, and would then it had bene publi=
shed, but I am the gladder it hath bene
stayed vntill this time, wherein so well a
learned gentilman, in ye Græke & Latine
tongues, & trauailed in certain vulgares,
sir Thomas Smith knight, hath written
his minde, touching this matter, in hys
booke of late set forth in Latin, entituled,
De recta & emendata linguæ Anglicæ
scriptione. Wherof and of this my trea=
tise, the summe, effect, and ende is one.
Which is, to vse as many letters in our
writing, as we doe voyces or breathes in
speaking, and no more: and neuer to a=
buse one for another, and to write as we
speake: which we must nædes doe if we
will euer haue our writing perfite: and
for such voices, soundes or breaths, as we
haue no fit Carrects, markes or letters,
we may without offence to God or reaso=
nable man, chuse and vse, fit new markes
or letters for euerye of them, and so we
maye be duely serued at our næde: and

not be driuen to abuse any one, in two or
three soundes, as we nowe doe diuerse.
Which I finde as reasonable as if a
Player of a Comedie or Tragedie,
woulde appoint the partes of the father,
mother and childe, to be played all by one
person, vnder one cote and gowne, and
one name, I confesse the beholders sight
shoulde be the lesse troubled with diuers
shapes and colours, or with diuersitie of
their names, but what a confusion, and
how much it woulde hinder the audience
from the sense of the matter (though the
personage could well counterfeit three di=
uers boyces) I report me vnto you: yet
by custome they maye vnderstande the
matter, after often seeing and hearing
therof.

Herein shall be shewed you, the aunci=
ent vse, power and sound of euery letter,
by cramples in diuerse languages, and
which letters, and how, they are by vs
and certaine other nations abused, so as
such as doe vnderstand the sayde langua=
ges shall nothing doubt therof.

Historics do show vs, that the Hebrues
(being

(being the most auncient nation) corrup=
ted their speaches and writing whyles
they were captiues in Babilon.

And that the Romaines, gouerning in
maner the whole worlde , constreyned
such of euery nation of their subiection,
as they would vse to deale with, for their
trafficke and affayres, to learne, vse and
exercise the Romaine or Latine tongue
and writing, the best they coulde, though
rudely and much corrupted , the Ro=
maines tooke paines therewith , rather
than to be driuen to learne the forren and
vnruled maner of speach and writing,
which they termed barbarous,as we, the
French, and others , doe account of the
Welch and Irish tongues:In whose ma=
ner of writings, peraduenture there is
better order kept, than anye of vs afore=
sayd doe.

And in like maner, the Romaynes af=
terwards,being inuaded by the Gothes,
Uandaloys, Lumbardes and Frenche=
men, by successe of time , chaunged their
ruled Latine to a vulgar Italian, which
is also now much differing from the be=
ginning

ginning o; firſt hundzed yeares vſe ther=
of, as in ſpeach, ſo in wziting.

Whereby you may vnderſtand, that
euery nation doth frame hir ~~toung~~ to hir
ſpeach the beſt ſhe may, accozding to the
right vſe of letters : which the moſt vali=
ant and ſtout champion and maintayner
of vſe and cuſtome, can not denie : as I
ſhall immediatly hereafter ſhewe you by
their weake reaſons and argumentes
which they are accuſtomed to make : and
how they haue bene and may be aunſwe=
red. And that in this pzeſent maner of
wziting, vnto the end of the vj. Chapter,
whereby you maye be ſufficiently pzepa=
red, to reade that which ſhall thereafter
folow in my purpoſed new maner: which
is pzinted with certaine ſuch new figures
o; letters as I could beſt deuiſe, both rea=
dye fo; the hande to wzite, and eaſie to
pzint, and that, to ſhow you therperience
fozthwith, of the eaſe and commoditie
therof. Which I doubt not, but the trac=
table will with an vpzight iudgement
read, and take a little paines to accuſtome
himſelf to the due ſounds of euery vowel,

Diph=

Diphthong and Consonant for the first
two or three leaues, and as he shall see
cause so to doe, and who so list not, he is
at his choyse to leaue. And doe desire no
further that any man should vnderstand
my sayd purpose, than as he may thinke
to take some profite thereof, whereof I
woulde be glad, and sorye to offende
any man, especially any reasonable and bertuous man,
for the rest, who can
auoyde their
murmu-
rings.

Vale.

C.j.   What

What letters are, and of their right vſe. The firſt Chapter.

IF I ſhould write of the inuenters of letters, wherein Authours are ſo variable, you might ſaye I followed their vncertaintie , which though we knew, I ſee not what pleaſure oꝛ pꝛofite it mought do vs. Wherfoꝛe it ſhall be ſufficient to vnderſtand (as experience teacheth vs) that the inuentoꝛs of letters whatſoeuer they were, had a regard to mans voyce : conſidering how many diuerſe ſimple wayes he might vſe his tongue and lippes with his voice in his ſpeach , which haue bene called Elementes, and that fitly. Foꝛ as the foure Elementes are the matter and ſubſtance of all thinges that are made in bodies and ſhapes, ſo are the ſimple voyces the partes, whereof the whole and round woꝛd and ſentences are compoſed and made. Foꝛ the noting and marking wherof, certaine men in diuerſe and ſundꝛie peoples and nations haue inuented

varia-

variable kindes of letters, ech with their perfite difference for euerye differing voyce: whereby it appeareth that as the voyces in speaking doe make a worde, so the letters shall doe the like in writing: seeing the voyces are as Elementes and the letters their markes and figures. The simple voyce is the least part or member of a speach, and the letter wee may wel call a maner of painting of that member for which it is written, whose quantitie and qualitie is presented to the understanding thereby, and so the diuers members of the speach ought therfore to haue eche his seuerall marke. Whereby is gathered that euen as euery body is to be resolued into those Elements whereof it is composed, so euery word is to be undone into these voices only whereof it is made. Seeing then that letters are the figures and colours wherewith the image of mans voice is painted, you are forced to graunt the writing should haue so many letters as the speach hath voyces, and no more nor lesse: so that if it be founde otherwise, for the abusion and falsenesse

C.ij.   thereof

Litera Elementi pictura; & nota.

Elementu in voce.
Litera in scripto.

Quot elementa tot sint litere.
Sua cuiq; elemento litera.

Scriptu ~~the~~ sermo pictus.

Litera, imagines vocu articulataru.

Tot litera quot voces./

Two faltz in th'Alphabet 1. One letter for diuers elements.
                          2. Diuers letters for one element.
Example of the 1/c. for k. e s./g. for yam & jod. ee
                2/c e s./g. e i./

An Orthography.

therof it is to be refused. Of which minde was Quintilian, as it appeareth in the rij. Chapter of his first booke, noting the custome of abused writinges, when he sayeth . Ego (non quod consuetudo obtinuerit) sic scribendum quicque iudico quomodo sonat. Hic enim est vsus literarum, vt custodiant voces, & velut depositum reddant legenti-bus.Itaque id exprimere debent quod dicturi sumus. Which signifieth , I doe not allowe that which custome may haue obtained. But doe iudge that all thinges ought to be written as it soundeth. This truly is thuse of letters, that they shoulde keepe the boyces and yeelde them againe vnto the Readers as a pawne or gage trusted vnto them to that ende: So they ought to expresse that which we woulde say. You see that Quintilian woulde haue the writing to be framed to the speaking, and howe the letter ought to keepe the boyce, and not to be yole , vsurped in sound or to be misplaced. Which disorders euery nation and people must of necessity leaue and forsake, if they will haue their

wri

Scriptura iuxta sonum, non sonus iuxta scripturam.
Subaudi
Comprobo.

Likeræ custodiunt voces.

writing perfite, easie , and pleasant to be
read. Which compasse they must take,
and vse as infallible and certaine, to lead
them the right course to be brought into
the desired hauen, I meane into the most
perfite way of writing , assured from all
offences of rockes or sandes, in reading,
whatsoeuer variable blastes of contrary
windes rooted in abuse, may rise agaynst
them to driue them therefrom. It must be
our weight and measure, touchstone and
fire to proue our writing, & thereby to trie
with a perfite sight & iudgement whether
it be such as we may find therin the same
number of letters in writing which wee
vse of voyces in speaking , without anye
scrupulositie, of custome, time, deriuation or difference, as shall be more at large
sayde hereafter, and that after thorder of
Phisicke, which is, first to vnderstand the
complexion , disposition and parts of the
body, and then to know the nature of the
causes which doe offende , whereby the
Doctor may proceede without daunger to
minister purgations of the vicious hu-
mors, with certaine remedies , and then

to preſcribe the pacient a wholeſome diet
and order to be preſerued from falling in=
to the like againe.

How ſome men maintaine our a=
buſed Engliſh writing.
The.ij.Chapter.

Owe before I open the
particular vices and abuſe
in our Engliſh writing , I
will recite the chiefeſt of
thobiections , which my
contraries vſe . Some of
them bring forth ſuch ſmal reaſons (worſe
than Corinths) as it were but labor loſt
to write them.

But others there are which maintaine
our ſuperfluitie of letters in writing with
foure arguments, wherein is ſome like=
lyhoode of reaſon.

Deriuation   The firſt is vnder pretence to ſhew the
deriuation and ſpring of ſome wordes bo=
rowed or taken forth of ſtrange tongues.

Difference
for words   Another is, that it ſhould be lawfull to
of one ſoud.   abuſe ſome letters to put a difference be=
twixt equiuoces or wordes of one ſounde.
                                                    The

Deriuation & Difference no iuſt cauſe, or why may not
me pen a is doubtfull as the eare, yia rather.

The thirde is for the time of vowels. *Time of vowels.*

But their strongest defence (which comprehendeth all) and that wherin they most triumph, is vse, wherof I will first speake generallye vntill I haue occasion by the perticulars. As I haue communed with some of them, first like friendes they would perswade me, not to speake of any misuse in our English writing, which (they saye) is of late brought to such a perfection as neuer the lyke was before. Yet I stayed not therewith fro my purpose, but woulde aunswere them partly with the reasons in my Preface. Then woulde they further replie, the power and soundes of some letters, haue bene ouer long double, for nowe to be receyued single, whatsoeuer they were aunciently: for that which vse by little and little and with long continuance bringeth into any peoples maner of doings, is neuer spoken or written against without great offence to the multitude : which will be ten folde more stiffenecked to receyue any newe letters, than a teame of wilde Steares would be at first to receyue the bearing of

Vse.

their

C.iiij.

their yokes. Though therperience should
proue it to be verye beneficiall to their
posteritie, so much they are offended at
all innouations. Wherefore you may doe
well to deport you from further speaking
therof. Such discouragings woulde they
vse, as others yet doe, and I know will,
as men grieued at the amendment of a=
ny thing.

Yet you may sée, they cannot deny, but
plainly confesse the vices in the corruption of the sound of letters, which we haue
in vse, for want of others to signify the ful
number of our boyces, and how they are
but crept in amongst our predecessours,
long since the first inuention of letters,
which therefore may the better be spoken
against : otherwise all sinne and vice
which is naturally in the fleshe, and of
longest vsed, ought not by their reason to
be spoken against, yet they may say, we
haue the law of Nature in our harts, and
the commaundement of God, written to
teach vs what we ought to doe, and leaue
vndone. So say I, that like as the law of
nature in our hearts, and commaunde=
ments

mentes of God written, doe teache vs a
purenesse of life to repzesent the nature of
God, wherfoze he created vs: so ought
the law of Reason which is in vs, to turn
our handes to ozder iustly, those figures
and letters which we shal make, to repzesent the voyces of our pzonounciation,
wherfoze we wzite them: & not to vsurpe
others powers, oz be ydle in their owne:
oz foz want of better example of our pze-
decessozs, to poztraict a monstrous figure,
wanting such members as are manifest
in the voice. Foz such an abused and vicious wziting, bzingeth confusion and vncertaintie in the reading, and therefoze is
iustly to be refused, and the vicious parts
therof cut away, as are the ydle oz offen-
siue members, in a politike common
welth: oz of trées oz vines, in any mans
ground: and other fruitfull and seruice-
able receyued, fauozed, and conueniently
set in their places. Further maye they
saye, though it shoulde be neuer so pzofi-
table, and allowed of al those learned and
reasonable men, which woulde take the
paines to reade your reasons, and thinke

well of them : yet the common people, wil
assone receiue a new maner of speaking,
as of writing of that they speake : and
therefore it is but winde lost, to speake of
any vse of letters in single soundes, sæing
they are receiued, and allowed for double
or treble : or of anye contentation, to re=
cepue any new figures, or knowledge of
Accentes, sæing we are contented with
the present maner now accustomed. Yet
can I not be so disswaded, in hope it may
like the learned and reasonable, or at least
giue them occasion to put pen to the pa=
per, for the amendment of our present er=
rors: according to the saying of Cicero in
his Paradoxis ad M.Brutum. videlicet.
Nihil est tam incredibile, quod non
dicendo fiat probabile: nihil tam hor-
ridum, tam incultum quod non splen=
descat oratione, & tanquá excolatur.
Which signifieth, there is nothing so in=
credible, but by declaration may be found
probable : nothing so terrible, so rough
and vnfruitfull, but by reasonable per=
swasion maye be clensed, made pleasant
and profitable. And a little after, Cicero
decla=

declaring that he tooke in hande to speake of those things, which the Stoikes did in no wise allow of, and by the way of pastime, to treate of certaine common places, which (bicause they were maruelous oʒ straunge, and against the opinion of al men) they called Paradoxa. Which he purposed to pʒoue, what effect his sayings might take: and that it might be tried, what difference there was betwixt a learned and a vulgar perswasion. Which Paradoxa he pʒoued true, thereby shewing what learning was able to doe amongst the rude multitude.

Tongues haue often chaunged (as it is sayd in the Pʒeface) then if occasion in the fancies of men, haue had power to chaunge tongues, much moʒe Reason should coʒrect the vicious wʒiting of the speach, wherein (as in all thinges) vse shoulde none otherwise take place, than experience pʒoueth it to be reasonable and pʒofitable, and the contrarie to be taken foʒ abuse oʒ misuse. And therefoʒe hath mankinde the vse of Reason (aboue dumb beasses) to searche the knowledge of the

D.ij.   meanes,

meanes, to lyue in a perfection, and to do
all thinges as he ought for his welth.
Which whosoeuer shoulde goe about to
resist, may be right well accounted to be
enimie both to God and mankinde. Then
let them resist and swell, as their nature
is: yet shal it be as easie for them to make
the seas faire medowes, as to make naturall thinges to be founde vnnaturall, or
conuert the nature of vice to be vertue in
dæde, what faire face or shewe soeuer it
may beare. Wherefore as wisedome biddeth vs to continue in such of our olde fa-
shions, or in others newly inuited, which
doe leade vs easily and without confusion, to that But and ende, wherbnto we
purpose , and to reproue those which
should bring troubles and lets in the way,
to a confustble and bncertaine maner of
doing: so when we maye amende eyther
newe or auncient maner, from the trouble and bnperfection of them, I thinke
that a verie little head (if it be not wholy
pole) will say, that their iudgement is of
very foly or madnesse, which shall speake
against the plaine and perfite way to the
ende

ende pretended. And that we ought to haue none other respect vnto our late cus= tomes, or those whiche we holde of long times, or séeme to be from euer, then as they shall be agréeing to reason and expe= rience: which ought to rule all thinges. Now that I haue written of vse in gene= rall, here followe the particuler vices which may be in writing: in such order as the course of the matter doth lead, where= in I shall shew their defences made for deriuation, difference and time.

Of the diuers vices which vse main-
   taineth in our writing, and how
      they are particularly by
         reason confuted.
            Cap.iij.

Writing may be corrup= ted foure wayes.
The first is by diminu= tion.
The seconde by superflui= tie, & that thrée wayes,
videlicet, for time, deriuation, and dif= ference.

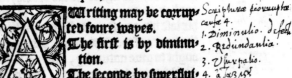

Scripturæ corruptæ causa 4.
1. *Diminutio. defect*
2. *Redundantia.*
3. *Usurpatio.*
4. *à τάξις*

An Orthography.

The third is by usurpation of one letter for another.

And the fourth and last, is by misplacing and disordering of them.

Of diminu-
tion di-
uersly.

For the first, a diminution is, when a writing wanteth sufficient markes, for the voices of the speach, whereby the writer is forced to usurpe one figure in two or more voyces, as a vowell to be made to serue in two soundes, eyther of two vowels, or of vowell and Diphthong, or any one Diphthong or double sounde, to be written for the longer time of one simple voice or sound of a vowell: or any vowell to be abused in thoffice of a consonant: or for anye consonant of one shape, to bee made to supplie thoffice of two voices or sounds: or the figure of the breath, to be applied to any one consonant, to make hir lose hir accustomed sounde, whereas the figure of the Aspiration, doth giue (or ought to giue naturally, and as it behoueth) us knowledge onely, when anye vowell or Diphthong should haue a harder breath before or after it, then by the reason of hir proper shape she ought to haue.

haue. All which faults, by reason of want of proper letters, we doe commit: whereby the Reader is brought to great doubts: as shalbe more at large said herafter.

Secondly, a writing is corrupted when any worde or sillable hath more letters, than are vsed of voyces in the pronunciation: whereby also ŷ writing must needes be false: & cause to the vnerpert that voice to be pronounced in reading, which is not in the worde in speaking. This abuse is great: partly without profite or necessitie, and but onely to fill vp the paper in writing: or the Compositors line in printing: to make a garnishing or furnishing therof with superfluous letters, to satisfie the eye to another ende than it ought: or the fancies of others for deriuations and differences: and partly vppon a reasonable cause, which is for time, when the vowell shoulde be longer sounded in one place than in another: which I confesse we are forced to doe, and is necessary, so long as we vse to double our vowels for other soundes than their owne, and will not vse to double them, for the longer

D.iiij.   quan-

Of super-
fluitie three
wayes.

Redundantia litterar
fluxus litteræ q̃ soni.

Comptroller.
Bloudde.
Adde.
Speake.

Causæ 3.
Tempus.
Deriuatio.
Differentia.

First, for
time of
vowels.

Vocales longæ & breues distinguendæ, notulis aut characteribus

quantitie of their proper sounds, nor doe so much as to vse a marke to signifie the same longer time : as other perfite writings of other tongues haue. But for deriuation or difference, there is neyther necessitie, nor commoditie to driue vs therebnto in any respect: and for time, I trust there is sufficient remedie in my new maner of writing : thereby to be eased of the abuse wherin we now are. For the opinion to maintiane a certaine superfluitie of letters, to shew the deriuations of wordes from any straunge language into ours, it is euen as we would not haue any straunger to be conuersant, nor dwell amongst vs, though he be a free Denison, and is fully bent to liue and die with vs to thend of his life:except(of a certaine fond curiositie)he should weare continually some mark,to be knowe whence he is, I think, to thend we should be able to know thereby how to refuse him when some of vs listed. Otherwise if he may be accounted as one of ours? Why shoulde he not be framed in euery condicion as we are? that is, to shew himself, appeare

and

Secondly, for deriuation.

Verba & dictiones deriuatæ ab alienis adaptandæ sunt idiomati mutuanti.

and be in very déde, naturall in euerye
condition, as wée are, and leaue all his
colours, or markes of ſtraungeneſſe, for
ſo the French doe terme it, when any forren is ſo receiued amongſt them, they cal
him naturallized. Yet will my contraries ſay that it is méete to be ſuperfluous
in writing, firſt for the knowledge whére
the word is deriued: and beſides, that we
are bound, to leaue ſome letter or letters,
in the words which we borowe of other
tongues, though we ſounde them not: to
be as of duetie, for a continuall knowled-
ging and remembrance, of the profite receyued: euen as euery Gentilman is
knowne by his armes, which are duelye
belonging to him. Yet haue they ſayd little for the purpoſe, except they can certifie
vs, how we are bound vnto it, and of the
profite of ſuch méerneſſe and conuenien-
cy of writing of any ſuperfluous letter, to
know whence ẏ word is deriued, as men
are by their armes. Firſt if it were conuenient or méete, it is for ſome profite, we
ſhould receyue therby in vſing it: or to a-
voyde ſome diſpleaſure or loſſe in leauing

*For know-
ledge.*
*Or bound
as of duety.*

*If conueni-
ent either
for profite,*

C.j.   it,

it, as for the profite, we sée none, but contrarywise great discommoditie, in disordring our writing from our pronunciation: to the great let, trouble & hinderance, both of the writer and reader. Secondly, if there mought come any displeasure, by leauing it vndone, it must be ministred by those nations, whose words we so borow: and that vpon a malice conceyued against vs for writing of their speach, otherwise than they doe. Such like (worse than brute) fantasies if any people had, I think they woulde be much more cholerick, for mispeaking of their speach, than for miswriting thereof: for that it maye much more offend them: as when a smatterer of their speach shoulde talke vnto them, so as they coulde not thereby conceyue his intention, rather than if his writings were giuen them, wherein the wordes which we haue borrowed of them were not written with some difference, more after their vse than our pronunciation. For if all their words therein were written thorowly as their owne hande would, yet without vnderstanding of the

Or to eschue displeasure.

rest,

rest, which shoulde be for our mother
tongue, they shall so well know what the
matter meaneth, as I knowe the great
Turkes thoughts. Wherfore if any people, could be angry with this matter, they
should much sooner be grieued, with the
otherwise speaking than the otherwise
writing: yet of neyther, I thinke any
people were euer so enuious as to com-
plaine. And for the reason of armes, there
is no such conueniencie or duetie in writing of a straunge word, for lyke as euery
straunger that any Prince recepueth to
be imploped in his seruice, what armes
soeuer his house doth giue, he beareth
notwithstanding the generall marke
wherwith the Princes naturall subiectes
are knowen from his aduersaries: so
ought the straunge worde (of what language soeuer) haue the generall and perfite marke of the Idiomate, whercinto it
is receyued, euen as in speach, so in writing. And like as two Gentlemen Aliens
of one house and armes, may seeke their
aduentures, and serue two Princes eni-
mies, and differ their conditions, so

C.ij. much

Verba mutuata;
praeter originis
suae notam; etiam
idiomati mutuanti
sunt quadranda.

much from their naturall , as the time and maner of the countrie shall minister occasion, and that without reproche of any reasonable man : so may euery nation vse others words, as they maye best frame their tongue therevnto , the writing whereof ought to be accordingly, without any scrupulositie. Thus we see no meetenesse or conuenience , for the obseruing of superfluous letters in deriuations.

If by bonds, they are eyther by the law of nature, or by consent.

Now let vs vnderstande what bondes we be in, if we be bounde, it is eyther by the law of nature, or by some maner of agreement of peoples one with thother. As for the law of nature (which is to doe as we would be done vnto) I trust there is none English man but would be contented that any nation should borowe of our language part or all : and vse it both in their speach and writing, as they mought best serue and please themselues therewith . What should it grieue vs? but euen as the shining of the sunne vpon any other countrie besides ours. And for any bonde or agrément betwixt peoples, you know

know well there hath bene none such, if
there had, it should haue bene but vnrea-
sonable and cruell. And further, it should
haue bene general for all words borowed,
of what tongue soeuer, as well as for a
fewe borowed of some tongues. Then
should we haue written yet much worse
than we now doe : for the substance of our
tongue, is deriued from the Dutch or
Saxon tongue : from which we differ in
our writing (and that necessarilye) so
much, that the French tongue written,
is as easie to the Saxons as our English,
or the French or Saxon to vs : wherefore
more méete it is, we should so differ from
them to our iust pronunciation (and that
aswell in all words borowed of whatsoeuer tongue) than to write as they doe,
wholy or partly from our speaking. For
any affection we haue vnto deriuation,
what coulde we varie from our pronunciation in these words: Thou hast a good
grandfather, except we would write the
verie Saxon tongue as thus, Du habst
ein gut groszvatter. The like is it for
Mother, Brother, Sister, Sonne, and
C.iij.   Daugh-

Daughter. Which they write, Mütter,
Brüder, Schwester, Son, vnd Toch-
ter, and infinite other simple words, as
such as vnderstande the tongue, doe well
know. And many sentences so néere, as
we knowe not what other order to vse,
then to write them the best we can as we
speake them, except we woulde write the
Saxon it selfe, as thus, a naturall Brother by Father and Mother wil liue with
brotherly loue, ein natürlicher Brüder
von Vatter vnd Mütter, wil láben mit
Brüderlich lieb. Wherefore shoulde we
be any more scrupulous, in the writing of
any words deriued from other tongues,
than we are of those? Some thinke the
Scottish speach more auncient Englishe
than as we now speake here in England,
yet there is no liuing English man, so
much affected to write his English as
they doe Scottish, which they write as
they speake, and that in manye wordes,
more neare the Latine, from whence
both we and they doe deriue them, as
fruct for fruit, and fructfull for fruitfull,
disponed for disposed or distributed, humne-
ly

ly for humbly, nummer for number, pul-
der for pouder, saluiour for sauiour, and
compt for account, and diuerse others,
wherein we pronounce not those letters
which they do, & therfore write them not
as reason is. Yet in others we do excæde
with them, as the b in doubt, c and h
in authoritie, l in souldiour, o in people,
s in baptisme, p in corps, and in condemp-
ned, and certaine like. And whereas of
this worde Campus, for the place where
an host of men doe lie, is sayde of the
French, le caump, of vs and the Scottes
men, the camp, yet doe we diuerslye deriue other wordes therefrom of one sense
as the French doe call the fields of corne,
les chaumps, and a good warriour vng
chaumpion, which we write and saye, a
champion, but the Scots men campioun.
The French sayth, *eschappe*, the Scots,
chapit, and we, scaped, whereby you may
sæ there is no cause for deriuation to vse
any superfluous letters in writing, when
as the voice is not spoken.

Then for difference, which is their last
defence, wherwith they maintain excesse
Thirdly, for difference, of and that

C.iij.

An Orthography.

for two causes.

of letters in writing, they pretende it conuenient for two causes: the first is for a

To know words of one sounde.

knowledge of equiuoces, which are words of one sound in speaking, yet signifying diuerse things, and woulde seeme therby to correct the nature of the speach, with their pen, thinking that by their letter added, at their discretion, the reader shall haue the better vnderstanding, for which thing it must be taken. As in this sentence, a hat for my sonne to keepe him from the burning of the Sunne, where is written o for the Boy, to be knowen not to be ment the Planet Sunne, which is written truly as we sounde it: and as we sounde the Boy also, and therefore ought so to be written. For being so written, who (seeing the sentence) will any more doubt of the true meaning thereof, then when he shall heare it spoken. As of this part of difference, I shall write more at large after I haue briefly shewed you the two other vices of vsurpation of powers and misplacing of letters. But first, of

For Etymologie.

thother difference which they say, is for a help to the vnderstanding of some words, simple

simple and others compound, by writing
some letters, which we vse not to sounde
in speach, and therfore to differ from the
speach, which is called Etymologie, seu
Veriloquium, & of others Originatio.
Whom I aunswere thus, Etymologie
doth by circumstance expound and make
plaine, the reason wherfore the worde or
name of thing is so called, as if you would
knowe why twentie, thirtie, fortie, fif-
tie. &c. be so called, I may aunswere, the
Etymologie is twaine tens, three tens,
fowre tennes. &c. which we vse to speake
and write notwithstanding, as before
sayd, and vnderstand thereby what num-
bers they meane in speach and writing,
and for the riuer of Tems, is wel known
what I meane writing it so, without any
nœde to write Thame-Isis, ech sillable
being (as I haue heard) the names of two
seuerall riuers before they ioyne. And so
the writer ought to be carefull, to write
euery word as it is spoken : maintaining
his Orthographie, as some other vulgar
nations doe : and as the Latines did. As
for example, what other letter, will any
F.J.   man

Etymologia.
Veriloquiū.
Originatio. /

man take vpon him, to adde (for any affection he hath to Etymologie) to this
worde Lepus, then euen so as it hath ben
left vs by the Latines, although it be (by
circumstance) of many expounded , (and
the reason therof giueth it) to be quasi le-
uipes, vel quasi leuem habens pedem.

And this worde, Heralt , is wholy a
Dutch word compounded of Herr , and
Alt, which is olde Maister, according to
the saying of Æneas Siluius , Erant au-
tem heroes veterani milites : yet some
doe compounde it with one Dutch word
and another French, writing Herhault,
signifying a high Maister , but the Etymologie of the worde doth proue it to be
Herralt and not Herhault. Notwithstanding, he should haue a wrong opinion of
me, that should thinke by the premisses,
I ment any thing shoulde be printed in
London in the maner of Northerne or
Westerne speaches : but if any one were
minded at Newcastell vppon Tine, or
Bodman in Cornewale, to write or print
his minde there, who could iustly blame
him for his Orthographie, to serue hys
                                            neygh-

neyghbours according to their mother
speach, yea, though he wrate so to London, to whomsoeuer it were, he could be
no more offended to seé his writing so,
than if he were present to heare him
speake: and there is no doubt, but that the
English speach, which the learned sort
in the ruled Latin, togither with those
which are acquainted with the vulgars
Italian, French, and Spanish doe vse, is
that speach which euery reasonable English man, will the nearest he can, frame
his tongue therebnto: but such as haue no
conference by the liuely voice, nor experience of reading, nor in reading no certaintie how euery letter shoulde be sounded, can neuer come to the knowledge
and vse, of that best and moste perfite
English: which by Gods grace I will the
neérest I can follow, leauing manye an
Inckhorne terme (which I could vse) bicause I regarde for whose sake I doe it.
Thus I cease to speake any further of
the vice of superfluitie. Nowe the thirde
vice, which may be in a writing, & which
vse keépeth in ours, is to giue diuers

powers

What the best Eng-lish is.

The thirde corruption is by vsur-pation of powers.

An Orthography.

powers to one letter, to the vncertaintie
& confusion of the reader, as shall be sayd
fully of euery one of our abuses, of euery
letter at large in my new maner of writing hereafter. Yet for example presently,
as whe we write, ponder two gentlemen
came togither vpon two Gennets, to giue
the to my Lord. Is there any knowledge
in the writing, to giue a man to vnderstand, when to sound ÿ g, as we vse before
e, and i, and when as before a, o, and u: for
following our custome, we shoulde alwayes giue it one sounde before e, and i,
as in gentle and Giles. Our abuses are
as great in others, and therfore nœde fit
Carects or letters, which we yet haue
not in vse : as shall hereafter appeare.
Where I nœde not to vsurpe, any one
letter or breath one for another.

The fourth corruption is by misse-placing.   Last of al, a writing may be corrupted,
by misplacing of letters, which we also
vse (I should say as of the others abuse)
and that most, in the finall sillables, ending in r, or l, aspired in pronunciation,
where we write the e, after, whe we pronounce it before, or no perfite e, at al sounded,

ded, as in ordze, bordze, numbze, rendze,
which haue bene well left of late dayes,
yet some such as would shew their knowledge of the french are curious therein,
and in trifle, hable, bedle, snaffle, buckle,
&c. Whereas in the first foure and such
like, the e, is better befoze, and nearest as
we speak it. And though y̆ french speak
it after, it is nothing to vs, foz we pretend
to wzite our speach and not theirs, but it
were much better (if it were in vse, & as J
doe vse, in my following new maner) to
consider that we in speach doe not sounde
fully two sillables, but one and an addition of a half sillable softly aspired, which
the r, doth alwayes take with it, & often
y̆ l, in our speach, as in y̆ last fiue wozds,
but no : in many other wozdes, foz which
difference we haue yet receiued no perfit
marke oz letter : which J doe hereafter
vse, foz the commoditie of the reader, and
therfoze did the inuentozs of letters call
l, m, n, and r, liquides oz semiuocales,
which signifieth halfe bowels, oz hauing
in maner the vertue of bowels. They
now foz lacke of better reason, will saye,

F.ij.   that

(margin note: Semisillaba.)

that who so hath the vse of our pronunciation, and will giue himselfe to reading,
shall not sticke at such trifles . I graunt
no lesse, but then he must first speake wel,
before he shall euer reade truely , and so
by learning to reade, he shall be nothing
holpen to attaine to speake well and truly. Hereby you maye sée how they closely
confesse that our writing is doubtfull and
hard, and that the reader must search his
remembrance, where he maye finde the
word more perfitely written than on the
paper. Thus trusting there is sufficiently
sayde, to proue that in our doings , we
ought none otherwise defende our selues
with vse, than as we shall finde it profitable and ioyned with reason . Yet will
not some of them be contented , but in
their malice (when they sée reason thus
assayle them) as men amazed , they will
stand and scolde vntill they be ouercome:
and saye, sée the vainglorious foole, who
thinketh himselfe to know more , and to
sée further , than other studious men,
which haue spent many yeares in learning, and yet finde no such faultes . To

them

them I aunswere, time trieth truth, and
though God hath giuen me this his gift,
is his worke therfore to be barked at: you
know God bestoweth his giftes diuersly,
to some one talent, to some another, non
omnia possumus omnes, and that all to
his glorie : wherefore they charge me
wrongfully with vainglorie, or any such
like. What are these raylings, other than
like as a man, seeing his enimie comming
towards him, strongly armed with his
weapon, and himselfe vnarmed without
weapon, and did not (as wisedome were)
prouide himselfe with armour and wea-
pons, meete for his defence : but stande
scolding, and aske whether he thought to
be able to ouercome him. In like maner
is it follie, so like ignoraunt men at their
wittes ende, to rayle at him that shall
reasonablye speake against any disorder
and abuse in what fashion of liuing soeuer
it be : when they should debate the matter
perticularly, and by the small rootes. Yet
thus doe some of them, which would be
taken for wise and learned men, and that
in the sciences : thinking that any lear-

F.iiij.　　　　ning,

ning, which is set forth by any other man, than by some one of themselues, though it be neuer so reasonable and true, should sound to their infamie and shame, if they should agrée thereunto: and that their obstinate opinion in ignoraunce and false learning, should appeare to be great wisdome, and therefore thought honorable.

Againe of difference.

Which sort, doe cause me yet to say somwhat more, touching our superfluous writing, for the difference of wordes of one sound. Some of them will saye, it is necessarie to put difference in wordes of one sound: least the reader should gather

Scriptura imago uocis.

Quæ sono sunt eadem, sit & scriptione.

a misse vnderstanding of them. If that were true, we should by like reason, vse a cackling and chattering, in steade of plaine speaking: for as they say, it is necessarie to write different letters, that the reader should not vnderstande amisse, so say I, that it is néedefull for the reader, to pronounce the same difference of letters written, least the audience, for want of hearing therof, should fal into the same doubt, which they say the Reader should doe by sight, if they were not written.

Thus

Thus you see by their obseruing of diffe=
rences, we should be conſtreyned to ſpeak
a farre other ſpeach and language than
we now do. That we may the better vn=
derſtand their minds, let vs conſider how
many differences there are in writing:
and we ſhall finde three. The one is the
common difference, when we write all or
ſome diuerſe letters to ſignifie diuers
things, as the earth, aire, fire and water:
& all things to mans knowledge or ima=
gination compounded of them: and this
differéce is ſo much, as euery mans hand
writing, doth ſomwhat differ frō another,
euen as do their faces, which is theffect of
their writing, firſt ſpoke of in the preface.

The ſeconde is, for the accident of the
voice ſpoken, whether it ſhould be long or
ſhort, ſharp or flat, ſpoken with a harde
or ſoft breath, and with as neare a know=
ledge as a mans hand may note, to mark
what voice ſhoulde be ſounded at ſome
time being written, and in another place
be left out, and the place marked to be
vnſounded: when the tongue doth vſe to
ioyne togither for diuerſe wordes, as

C.I.   though

First dif-
ference.

Vocū differentia
literas,

Voces differunt
literarū notis,
accidentibꝰ

Second dif-
ference.

Time.
Tune.
Breath.

Per Apo-
strophe.

Coniunc-
tion.

An Orthography.

though they were but one : and when the
writing mought else giue the reader cause
to sound some Diphthong or Triphthong,
when the vse of the tongue is to sunder
them into two sillables : that he may haue
an assured mark for the knowledge therof. And for distinction and pointing, to
giue the reader knowledge the nearest a
man may to pronounce the writing, as
the writter would speake it.

Of which accidentes I will write, for
the helpe of the ignoraunt of them : and
giue sufficient examples, before I enter
to the vse of them, togither with the
knowledge of the seuerall voices, which
are in our speache, with conuenient
markes or letters for those that we lacke.
Wherefore I will passe these other accidents till then, except the first, whereof
I thinke it meete to say somwhat presently. Which is for time long or short, as in
this sentence, Commonly ware is deare
in warre time, where we vse the finall
e, in ware, deare, and time, for the longer
quantitie of the preceding bowels, and
that with some reason, lacking a note for
the

Diuision.

E. in fine; signu;
vocalis congi.

the knowledge of that quantitie , but for
the shorter time of the a, in warre (to differ ware from warre, according as we
differ in speach) it is very vnreasonably
begun, and so continued, to adde another
sillable, to weete re, which we vse in infinite such like words, where there mought
appeare the same doubt: yet others with
some more reason, in such words doe only double the consonant without the e, as
in all, barr, and sadd . But both shoulde
be superfluous, vsing a knowledge for the
long vowell, and all other without that
marke to be knowen thereby to be short,
with the helpe, at some times, of the a-
cute accent , to signifie the shortnesse,
when any doubt might be , as by experience it may appeare vnto you, in my new
maner herafter. And for the longer quantitie of the vowell it had bene very well
(if our predecessors had kept the vowels
in their proper sounds) to haue vsed them
double therfore, which now in doubling
we sounde otherwise than in their owne
sounds.

But now this third and last difference,

rooted

rooted only in mannes wit, is that which
dissolueth our doubt : whereby a mans
iudgement, is able to decerne, the sundry
meaning of words, like as in hearing, so
in reading : by the reason and discourse of
the matter and sentence : and that not only, if they be written or spoken somewhat
amisse : but also though there were some
sillable lacking, other the thing (by dis-
tance of countries) otherwise named,
where it was written, than where it was
red. Wherefore, if difference were so necessarie as they saye, it were much more
needfull in the speaking than in the writing ; saing the speach passeth so quicklye
away, whereas the writing remayneth,
so as the reader may tosse and turne it, in
searching (by reason of the sentence) the
true meaning of the doubtful word. As in
these examples following, he was at the
Plough in Smithfield, with good Oxen,
and after at the Harrow with good horses, who so knoweth Smithfielde to be a
weekely market of horses, and all accustomed time of cattel, and signes to be made
with littell counterfet ploughes and Har-
rowes,

rowes, for knowledge of houses, shall
forthwith conceyue the writers minde:
euen as he mought if he had hearde him
speake. Also, well Boy I say beware the
well, it is deepe. And this great Beare
will beare ten dogges. And, Hodge Bill,
with his browne Bill, brought me a sea-
led Bill, and a Woodcocke by the Bill.
And, your horse bare a heauie lode, being
bare before. And many other equiuoces,
where we make no difference in speach,
& therfore ought we to make none in writing: though they be of diuerse significa-
tions, if now they coulde shewe me their
reason why they vse their fantasie in
some, and not in these foresayde and many more, agaynst the order of good writing, I would be glad to heare them. But
I know they cannot, except they woulde
saye (as the truth is) it is for feare, it
should be to easie for the Reader. This
wit and experience of man, is able to de-
riser and declare, the meaning of some
darke writings which he neuer sawe before, although there were vsed therein
great studie, that no man but such as had

G.iij.   the

the order of it, in minde or writing, should
be euer able to read it(As I haue heard of
one hath bene able to do) much more than
of that the writer is willing euerye man
shoulde read. By this we maye also perceyue, that superfluous letters to cause
the writing of a worde to differ from the
speach, for Etymologie, is in lyke maner
nothing necessarie nor commodious. Let
vs conclude then that though these obser-
uers of differences woulde neuer so faine
corrupt the order of writing in wordes of
one sounde, yet maye they not breake the
law of true writing. And that we abuse
not letters signifiyng voyces, for the
marke of time : especially when we may
(with pleasure) remedie it, as by experience is layde hereafter before your eyes :
and found more easie, short, profitable and
certaine. And that finallye (notwithstanding those fantasticall Sophisters, which
doe indeuour to maintayne our vicious
writing by their diuers defences)we must
be ruled by our speach : and euen as the
tongue doth chaunge thaccidents of voyces in place, time, tune, and number, so
we

we alwayes in our writing to chaunge
the markes, being the image of the voice:
euen as the Painter, ought to chaunge
the variable quantities and accidents, in
the images of the man, whose figures he
would counterfet, for euerye ten yeares
of his age. And now the better to call to
remembrance, the principall partes and
effect, of that which hath bene sayd, I wil
vse this Allegorie, and compare the liuely
body of our pronunciation, which reason
biddeth the writer to paint and counterfet
with letters, vnto a man, which woulde
commaunde an vndiscréete Painter to
portraict his figure, as thus: naming the
man Esop. Who cōming to a Painter,
sayth. Frend, I would haue thée to counterfet the quantitie and qualitie of my body and apparell, by thy craft, so liuely as
those men, which haue euen nowe séens
me, may know (whensoeuer they maye
sée it hereafter) that the same is made to
represent me vnto them, as I now am.

The Painter aunswereth: Sir stande
you there, and I shall doe it, as I vse to
doe others, and as all the Painters of

this

this countrie are accustomed to doe. E-
sope, howe is that? The Painter aunswereth. Though you weare hose and
shwoes, your figure shall nœde none. But

Deriua-
tion.

Diffe-
rence.

Etymo-
logie.

Length of
vowels.

For short-
nesse of
vowels
the double
consonants.

it shall therefore haue painted
other apparell, by a thirde more
than you weare, and vpon euerie seuerall pœce, I will marke
and write, the countries name
whence it came. And bicause
your clothes, as well the cloth
as the furre and silke, are of one
colour, I will make them to be
the better sœne of diuers colors.
I will also write in your fore-
head your fathers and mothers
name that men may see of what
stocke you are come of. Where
as in some countries Painters
doe vse to make the nose, of like
quantitie to that in the body, we
set others at the endes of them.
And for making the littlenesse
of the eyes, we make the compasse of ẙ head greater, than the
naturall, ⁊ double ẙ eie browes.
Then

Then in the place of eares, we doe vse to paint eyes.

And last of all, I will chaunge the middell fingers and thombes in others places. The Painter. How like you this, will it not doe well? Esope. Yes, but I would faine knowe, for what purpose: and the reason wherefore you woulde doe thus. The Painter. Bicause the Painters of this countrie, for time out of minde, haue vsed the like, and we continue therein, and bicause it is so commonly receyued as it is, no man needeth to correct it. A good aunswere. Nowe leaue we them, and I demaund the maintainers of such Painters of our pronunciatiō, if they had fortie or more of their portratures drawen, shaped and coloured of their foresaid friende: and those same set vppon the pillers of Powles Church, who should be able to know (but they themselues, being dayly vsed in naming them) which shoulde be for the one, or which for the other. For they shoulde not halfe so well represent them, as should the well proportioned figures of so manye skipping Babians,

H.i.   Apes,

3
Vsurpation of power.
4
Misplacing

Apes, Marmozets or Munkeys, and dauncing Dogs and Beares.

Better can not a writer be compared, than to a Painter: For, as neuer Painter coulde counterfet the liuelynesse of a man (though he behelde him all his lyfe) except he first considered all his lineaments and proportions, and knew the diuersitie of his colours: and vnderstode well, that one colour can not make two places of one hewe, to be of diuers coulours, what quantitie so euer he laye on. So was there neuer writer, ignorant of all the perticulars, of the boyces spoken, and that shall want due markes and colours for them: that could perfitely counterfet the pronunciation, though by vse (or better abuse) it were allowed. Wherfore, that the Reader may vse, the perfite waye in euerye Englishe word, which may be spoken (calling English all deriued words receyued, or which hereafter shall be) and be no longer troubled, in this disorder and abuse, to the confusion and trouble of the Reader, I will immediatly hereafter, shewe you all the voices,

voices, which our speach vseth, and so vse seuerall markes or letters for euerie one of them: with necessarie accents, and vse of pointing: and then I will put it in experience, in the rest of my treatise therafter.

Of the number of our vowels, and of their auncient sounds, in which they are alwayes vsed, in the new maner hereafter: by which their perfite vse, our present abused sounds of some of them, are founde to be Diphthongs.

Cap.iiij.

Vocalin̄.
Numeras.
Sonus.

Owe that there is sufficiently sayde what letters are, and of their right vse, and of the vices which some doe maintaine in our English writing, so as me thinkes euery reasonable man may be aunswered therewith: I shall briefly in this Chapter shewe you what voyces, sounds and breaths we vse in our speach, and accordinglye vse one simple and sole

propositum.
+ hereafter

H.ij.   figure

An Orthography.

figure for ech one of them: much differing
from the disorder & confusion we now are
in, and that by forgetting and leaving all
superfluous letters vnvsed, and calling to
minde, and taking of others fit & commodious for vs, with sufficient examples of
their due, sole, and onely sounds. And af-
terwards of the accenting, and pointing,
wherein the rest of this treatise is written. As touching the divers soundes and
noyses, which are & may be by inanimate
things, nor of such soundes and voices as
are made of brute and dumbe animals,
they doe nothing appertaine to this purpose : but only of the reasonable speach of
mankinde, and especially of our English
tongue : which speach reasonable is made
with divers organes and instrumentes,
namely, the breath from the Lungs or
Lights, Arteries, Throte, Vuula, mouth,
Tongue, Teeth and Lippes, but such of
them as doe give vs the most distinction
and perfite sense, of the sounde or breath
given, are the tongue, the teeth and lips,
by their divers vse and feelings or tou-
chings in and of the mouth.

Wher-

Wherefore I will forthwith shew you
their figures, in such wise, as with our
passed, and yet our present maner of Or-
thography, you may vnderstand by what
voice or breath euery one letter is vsed in
the .vij. Chapter, and the rest of this treatise hereafter . Where I shall further
treate with more ample reasons & autho-
rities, than is done in this maner of writing, why their figures should be proper
vnto them : by reading wherof you may
finde by experience the manifest commodities before sayd . First I finde that we
vse fiue differing simple soundes or voyces, proceding from the brest, without
any maner of touching of the tongue to
the palet or foreteeth, or of the lippes close
ioyning togither : or eyther of the lippes
to their counter teeth. Their due and auncient soundes, may be in this wise verye
sensibly perceyued : the first , with wyde
opening the mouth, as when a man yau-
neth : and is figured a. The seconde, with
somewhat more closing the mouth, thrusting softlye the inner part of the tongue
to the inner and vpper great teeth, (or

H.ij. gummes

Vowells.

The tongue indeed
toucheth not the
foreteeth, but it tou-
cheth the back teeth.
m a . e . i .
nor the lips do touc
their counter teeth
nor do they ioine
close togither, but
they are contracted.
a m o e u.

Robinson formes oth o E u with the tongue, far within the mouth.

e.

i.

o.

u.

gummes for want of teeth) and is marked e. The thirde, by pressing the tongue in like maner, yet somewhat more foreward, and bringing the iawe somewhat more neare, and is written i. The fourth, by taking awaye of all the tongue, cleane from the teeth or gummes, as is sayde for the a, and turning the lippes rounde as a ring, and thrusting forth of a sounding breath, which roundnesse to signifie the shape of the letter, was made (of the first inuentor) in like sort, thus o. For the fift and last, by holding in lyke maner the tongue from touching the teeth or gummes (as is said of the a, and o) and bringing the lippes so neare togither, as there be left but space that the sounde may passe forth with the breath, so softly, that (by their ouer harde and close toyning) they be not forced thorow the nose, & is noted thus u. And holding the top of your fingar betwixt your teeth, you shall the more sensiblye feele that they are so made with your sayd instrumentes. So you may consider how these fiue diuers sounds are distinctly made: yet some man may

i. rightly sounded in Italy. spaine. France. & wales. ie. ut ee noise,
Italy. france & spaine: confound up consonant & vowell under one char
acter. The welsh distinguish them V. for the consonant thy still write

An Orthography.

may doubt howe to sound part of them,
bicause they haue bene and are abu=
sed in diuers soundes : wherefore after J
haue sayde somewhat of them , J shall
shew you their auncient soundes, yet ge=
nerally vsed thorow all Dutchland ouer
and nether, in their vulgar tongues, and
in pronouncing their Latine , the like of
Jtalie, also of the French, the Spanish,
and Brutes for the a, e, i, and o. But these **welsh.**
three last named Nations do all abuse the
u, with vs in sounde : and also the Ger=
maine and Jtalian for the consonant ex=
cept the auncient Brutes which haue al= **Britaine.**
wayes continued this figure v, for the **v, consonant**
consonant, whose example J doe minde *The english sound*
to followe. And we our selues doe right= *ei, or ai for i.*
ly sound all fiue vowels in the Gospell in
Latine, In principio erat verbum.&c.
vnto sine : where i, is sounded the Diph=
thong ei, or Græke ei, & in qui,as though **ei, diph-**
it were written quei, whereas in quis **thong.**
and quid it is rightly sounded, also the
Gramarians selfe , which teache the
Grammer, doe fall into the fault of Iota=
cisme, which is forbidden them at the be=
H.iiij.   ginning,

ginning thereof: and doe pronounce the
same in these Pronounes following, and
infinite other words, as in ꝑ vocatiue mi,
they sound in mei or mei: mei they sound
mei or méei, whereas in mihi, many of
late days do sound the i, right in both sillables, euen as i, in nobis, the like true soūd
of i, they vse in tui and sui but wil not yet
frame their tongues to sound it so in tibi
and sibi as they doe in mihi, vobis, tuis,
and suis, ille, ipse, iste, hic, and is. Yet
in the declining of them they misname
the i, in the second sillable, as in illius, il-
li, ipsius, ipsi, istius, isti, and the like in
the Nominatiues plurall, but in the Da-
tiues and Ablatiues they can sounde it
right: which fault, none of all the nations before named, did euer commit, for
the i, bowell: but doe kéepe it still in one
sole ꝭ the auncient sound: euen as the naturall ꝭ artificiall Gréekes do their Iota:
which also did neuer make it consonant:
no more haue the Brutes, the Germains,
nor the Italians: which Italians haue
deuised for the sounde of consonant, the
gi, nor haue any of the other thrée nations

(as

(as farre as I can learne) that sounde of
gi in their speaches : as shall be sayd more
at large when I come to treate of g, yet
the French and Spanish with vs and the
Scots men, doe vsurpe the i, before a, o,
and u, as the g. before e, and i. And for
the Diphthong ei, many auntient Gram-
marians in borowing of Greeke wordes
haue put often i, alone, which the Germaine doth not allow : knowing them of
long continuance to be of diuers sounds :
and therefore when they thinke the ei,
moete to be sounded in such wordes as are
deriued from the Greeke, they write it so:
which whoso list may see, in a Latine and
Dutch Dictionarie, Authore Petro Da-
sypodio, entituled, Dictionarium la-
tino-germanicum, & vice versa Ger-
manico-latinum. And out of all doubt,
no nation of the foresaide but we and the
Scottish, doe at any time sounde i, in the
foresayde sounde of ei: Wherefore, that
English Greeke Reader which shall giue
the same sound to i, which he doth to ei,
doth further this errour much amongst
vs. Now to come to the u. I sayde the

I.I.   French,

French, spanish, &
litsh. e. scot: vse i.
sonant before a. o.

i. consonant

no nation but we
scots pronounce i
as we dm.

u, vowell.

An Orthography.

French, Spanish, and Brutes, I maye adde the Scottish, doe abuse it with vs in sounde, and for consonant, except the Brutes as is sayd: the French doe neuer sounde it right, but vsurpe ou, for it, the Spanyard doth often vse it right as we doe, but often also abuse it with vs: the French and the Scottish in the sounde of a Diphthong: which kéeping the vowels in their due sounds, commeth of i, and u, (or verie neare it) is made and put togither vnder one breath, confounding the soundes of i, and u, togither: which you may perceyue in shaping thereof, if you take away the inner part of your tongue, from the vpper téeth or Gummes, then shall you sound the u, right, or in sounding the French and Scottish u, holding still your tongue to the vpper téeth or gums, and opening your lippes somewhat, you shall perceyue the right sounde of i. But for the e, and o, I finde not that any of the sayd nations do abuse them as we do, except ꝑ French in the ou, for u, as is said (and that constreyned therevnto with vs, I must néedes saye, bicause they nor we haue

French, spanish.
welsh, english & scotz.
have this small u.

u: ought not ou
Galli
u: ut in: scotis.

iu, diph-
thong.

French e scotn u.
iu, diph-
thong redu-
ced into hir
elements.

haue vſed the u, and we onely the i, in their due ſounds) to call the e, in teaching the A.B.C. in the ſound of i, and to double the e, for that ſound, as in ſée the Bée doth flée. And o, ſingle or double in the ſound of u, as, they two come to do ſome good, which is the méere ſound of the u, As for the a, we doe little abuſe, wherefore I omit it in this place. And for the quantitie of bowels, I neuer minde to vſe the final e, making two ſillables in writing when one is ſpoken, but do borow the vſe of the Gréekes, which were wont to write their i, in the line after bowels which were long, and doe vſe it ſtill after great letters, as we doe the e, for the quantitie of the precéeding bowell. But nowe they write it vnder the ſmall, and in ſome printes is but euen a pricke, and the lyke may ſerue vs for the quantitie of bowels: which I vſe hereafter. And to perſwade you the better, that their auncient ſounds are as I haue ſayde, I report me to all Muſitians of what nations ſoeuer they be, for a, e, i, and o: and for u, alſo, except the French, Scottiſh, and Brutes

I.ij.   as

(margin)

e,

o.

u.

e, finall for time to be left.

as is sayd : for namely all English Musitians (as I can vnderstande) doe sounde them, teaching vt, re, mi, fa, sol, la : And so do all speakers and readers often and much in our speach, as in this sentence : The pratling Hosteler hath dressed, curried, and rubbed our horses well. Where none of the fiue vowels is missounded, but kept in their proper and auncient soundes : and so we maye vse them, to our great ease and profite. And for their longer time, it were more reason to double themselues, in the place where the quantitie and longer sounde is made, than to write the e, for it, at the ende of the sillable or worde, or to write a Diphthong in the middest for like longer time : whereas one vowell onely is sounded. For the word Diphthong signifieth a double sounde : and the vowels (thone takes not any part of the sound of the other) are made of sole and single or simple sounds : but for the sayd longer time, the pricke vnder will be most fit and conuenient. And as you are hereafter prouided for therin, so are you for the consonants b,

and

and *z* , so that you maye kæpe the fiue
vowels in their only figures and sounds :
as in these examples herebnder : so alwayes of our predecessors and the liuing
now still vsed.

| The aunci-ent and sole sounds of the fiue vowels are of | a e i o u | as in | Haue Adam. Set the net. Bring this in. No not so. Cum vp cut. |

Which is their due and proper sounds,
and as we our selues vse them when we
read Latine, as is sayd of In principio
vnto sine, and so thorow the Gospell except a few other words as the i, in vita,
vitam, viri, and qui some sounde it also
in ei, and the u, in lux we vniuersallye
sounde it right, but in lucet and lumine,
some vsurpe the French and Scottishe
sound, and also in fuit, cui and sui which
ought to be kept in one sounde in all
wordes, as in verbum, deum, ipsum,
sunt. &c . The onely sounde for vowels
of all the fiue : wherein the Italians and
Germaines, doe continue them vniuer-
sally through all their speach or writing :

I.iij.   is

is euen as we vſe them in the foreſayde
laſt eramples haue Adam.ɩc. As the Ita‑
lian doth ſounde them in this one worde
riputatione, and as the Spanyard doth
vſe them all, but the u, which he abuſeth
with vs and the Scottiſh , but not gene‑
rally as the French doe. And the Dutch
as in the firſt ſentence of the foreſayde
goſpell of Saint John. Im anfang was
das wort, vnd das wort was bey Gott
vnd Gott was das ſelbig wort , where
they are all ſounded as thorowe all their
ſpeach as the Italians doe , and as the
Spanyard and we doe often.But for con‑
ſonants I muſt confeſſe the Italian and
Germaine with vs , the French and
Spanyards doe abuſe the u, yet the Al‑
main neuer or ſeldome writeth the figure
u, for conſonant, but (with the Walſh)
thus v, and by negligence vſeth the ſame
alſo for vowell as in vnd, but not before
any vowell, where it might be taken for
a conſonant. And for the conſonant i, the
Italian hath founde it ſo vnmæte as he
hath prouided for it the vſe of gi,as is ſaid.

Thus truſting that you be certified of
the

the auncient and due soundes of the fiue vowels (I finde not that we shall næde any moȝe) wherein only we ought to vse them, and so as when two oȝ thȝæ of them may come togither the same and none other sound of ech must appeare: but that the sounde must be longer oȝ in a higher tune of the last than the first, oȝ the two first, if it be in a Triphthong, that is, of thȝæ soundes. Which come in our speach but seldome: but the Dipthong very often. And euery one may ioyne with any one of hir other foure fellowes, and be made a double sound as is sayd in one sillable, yet two vowels may also come togither, and the first haue hir full sounde as well as the latter, but then they make two sillables: foȝ the knowledge wherof, I doe vse ouer the latter vowell two pȝickes receyued in both Græke and Latin Dyæresis thus ¨. The high Dutch not *Dyeresis.* ¨
vsing alwayes one figure foȝ the vowell, and another foȝ the consonant of the u, do vse (as we from them) the double w, befoȝe ech one of the other vowels in Dipthong, foȝ which the Italian, French,

and

and Spanish, doe vse to write the g, before u, to cause the reader, to be certaine
that the v, is no consonant. The Dutch
doe vse also au, ei, and ie, rightly as I do
hereafter, and á, in the sounde of æ, or e
long: ŏ in the sounde œ, or eu : ü, in the
sound of iu, or the French and Scottish u,
ů, for eu, and ú for u, long, or French ou,
with other vowels before and after them,
which figures if næde were, we mought
haue borowed, but are ancipites and
doubtfull for the Reader, which is not in
those hereafter, where ech vowell is sæne
for hir selfe : as they are vsed in speach.
And so vsing the i, alwayes vowell as is
sayd, we shall neuer næde the y, wherevnto we giue the verie sounde of i, or ei,
nor the w, for that I will also vse, one figure for the consonant : and thother for
the vowell : and the pricke vnder for the
longer sounde. And for Diphthongs and
Triphthongs, I næde to giue none examples in this place, but doe deferre them
til I haue shewde you the figures and names of all our sounds and breaths. And in
the meane time I will giue you to vnderstande

ŏ. ü.

ü. ů.

y.left.

w.left.

ſtande which (of ſuch as we doe now vſe)
we doe vſurpe: for ſome of them , and
which we doe rightlye vſe : and giue you
examples of the, as is done of the vowels.

The number of conſonantes and
breathes, which we vſe in our ſpeach,
with the leauing of ſuperfluous letters, and receyuing of ſuch other
as we neede : with example
of their right vſe.

Cap. v.

I Finde that we doe vſe. xii.
diuers dumbe or dul ſounds
in our ſpeach, comming frō
the breſt with a breath as
it were gröningly, diuerſi-
fied eyther by touching of
the lippes togither, or of the vnder lippe
to the vpper tæth, or of the tongue to the
palet, to the vpper great tæth or gums,
or to the vpper foretæth : whereof ſeauen
of them haue as many felowes or ſiſters,
and may be ſo called, for that they are
ſhaped in the mouth in one ſelfe maner
and faſhion : differing only by leauing of

K.j.   the

the inward found, ↄ vſe but of the breath,
ſo as the one mought be allowed to ſtand
in place and paſſe muſters for hir felow,
euen as the females (of the neareſt like
vnto the males)of any kind,mought for ẏ
males, or contrarywiſe. The one couple

b. p.   or paire, is the b, and p.Another is the v,
v. f.   conſonant and f. Then g, and k, or c, as
g. k.   before a,o,and u, which c, ſæing the k,is
d. t.   ſo well knowen as it is, I had as liefe be
         beholding to t he Græke for their k, as to
c, left, and the Latine for their c, and to vſe the c,
k, receiued. with a, a differing note for the ſounde of
ch , for it is not the proper office of h, to
ſerue in that ſort,nor as we do with t, and
with s, for ſo euery conſonant is aſpired
and breathed : and no ſound can be made
in mans breſt without his breath though
it be kept in, as for b, g, d, ↄ m, though a
man dos ſtoppe his noſe and kæpe in his
breath, yet he may make the inwarde
ſound of them : which is by the meane of
his breath . And the conſonants may all
be framed and vttered ſenſibly to the eare
without the naming of anye vowell or
Diphthong : the maner whereof I can
not

not so well expresse by writing as by
mouth, but the nearest I maye, I shall
write hereafter. And we must be carefull
to sound the g, as ÿ Grecians do gamma,
the Hebrues guimel, as the english Sar-
ons did and yet is vsed in all Dutchlande
ouer and nether, and kept of the Brutes
or Walsh vnto this day, that is before e, &
i, as before a, o, and u: as we also often
rightly do: as in this sentence, leaue your
anger, and giue me your girdle to get
this togither: for which onely sounde, I
shall always vse the g, without any næde
of the h, betwixt the g, and e, or i, as the
Fleming doth. And for the sound of the j,
consonant, for which the Italian doth vse
gi, to be serued according to our nǽde, we
must take a newe figure, for which Sir
Thomas Smith hath chosen the English
Saron Ȝ and I doe vse the same hereafter, a little diuersifying the shape to differ
more from g, and to be readier for the
hande to write, thus ȝ: for which we
mought haue vsed also this marke j, but
the other is better, for that it nædeth no
pricke ouer it (which is the note of the i,

B.ij.

[margin notes:]

g in one
sound.
g: sieeu:

Græcis.
Hebræy
Saxonibus
Germanij
Cambris.

g: semper sieeu
ante a·o·u·
aliquando ante, e.i.

ȝ, for j, conso-
nant.
G, for ch.
j, consonant
to left.

An Orthography.

to be the better knowen before or after, or betwixt m, and n. And for the sounde of the li, I finde no fault. The fellow or sister of ʒ is the sound of þ Italian c, before e, and i, and of our and the Spanish most common sound of ch. For which the high Dutche doe wryte tsch, as in Teutsch, Teutscher, gehetscht, & Verdolmetscht. For which there mought be vsed, as we haue accustomed the ch, but that the truth is, as also Sir Thomas Smith sayth, the h, is in that sort much abused, for which sound of ch, he alloweth the c, before and after all vowels and diphthonges alike: and doth declare it to be the auncient soud of c, but bicause it hath bene so long and yet is of many nations with vs abused in two soundes, I thinke it better to receyue some other figure, for which I haue turned my penne (as for the others hereafter) diuers wayes, as thus, ch, cc and G, whiche last I finde the readiest for the hande, and to ioyne with the following letters best. Fifthly, this couple d, and t, which we vse rightly in reading English most commonlye, but manye doe abuse them

G, for ch.

d. t.

them in reading Latin in certaine words
in the sound of the following couple, as is
sayde at the beginning of the Grammer,
and shall be sayde in my newe maner.
Sirthlye we haue a paire of soundes for
which we doe vsurpe the th, alone, which
I, with Sir Thomas Smith, doe leaue,
and vse for eche one a diuerse figure: and
whereas he vseth for them the English
Saxon letters called the thorne ð, thus,
ð, or the Greeke Δ for thone, and the
Greeke θ, or Saxon þ for thother, I haue
followed the readynesse of the hande, as
is sayde for the ʒ, and ɢ, and haue deuised for this couple d, for the thorne ð, or
dh, ꝺ, for th. And the other paire which
we haue, is the ʒ, and s, and some thinke
the sh, shoulde be the s, aspired, which I
coulde not well auoyde, if I had not na-
rowly considered and founde the ʒ, and s,
to be shapen in one sort, which is with
thrusting the tongue to the palet, and
teeth or gummes forward, so as the first
is then sounded with a soft breath thorow
the vpper foreteeth, and hir fellow without any sound, and with a harder breath:

K.iij.   obser-

d, new.

ꝺ, for th.

ʒ. s.

*linguā ad vacies
dentium superior
applicati vires*

*ʒ: nixat leniter
ōnium mittit.
s. denum
extrui oni.*

ꝃ: linguam retrahit interius ad palatium: pirat denſum:

ſh.

The tongue is laid in all for the ſound of this letter

I like not this biting of the lip, it helps not mee to ſound this letter

It hath his owne b, is a iuſt conſone, wherfore he doth not will, to part it with h, & is call it a ſpirit.

obſeruing thozder of all the ſire other paires: wheras the huſhing of this bzeath is made thozow the tæth only and taking of the tongue from the palet, and dzawing it inward to the vpper gummes oz tæth: which you may perceyue by cloſing your tæth togither, and ſo thzuſting forth of your bzeath harde: oz by biting your vnder oz vpper lip, & thzuſting your bzeath thozowe your tæth, and ſo this bzeath is perſitelye made. By which doings you maye finde that the z, noz s, can not be made but by touching of the tongue to the palet. Foz the felowe of which ſh, the French do ſounde their g, befoze e, and i, and the i. conſonant befoze a, o, and u, and ſometimes befoze e, and doe neuer ſound perſitely our ſounds befozeſaid foz z & G, in all their ſpeach. Foz which ſh, I haue framed a new figure, with lyke regarde foz the ſhoztneſſe and eaſineſſe foz ꝩ wzi= ting, as foz the reſt befozeſaid, & is thus **ʃ**.

ʃ, for ſh.

Then we haue foure ſoundes of the li= quides oz ſemiuocales, l, m, n, and r, of

l, m, n, r.

which I muſt nædes confeſſe, as of ſome others befoze, to be rightly vſed in ſounde when

when they be single. Wée haue further
the l, aspired lyke to the Spanishe and
Walsh often vse of the ll, which maketh
the. rij. dumbe or dull sounde, but we vse
it not that I know of, at the beginning of
any words as they do : but often at thend
of words, as in this sentence, the bei le is
hable to sable. Where we wrest the e,
which is but closely or (as it were) halfe
sounded : wherfore we may with as smal
cost and labour, as of the rest, vse a fit figure for it : and neuer néede to vse the ll,
or lh, and for the reasons abouesaid not to
abuse the h, but as I haue in the other cō-
sonants aspired, vsed the least draught of
the penne, I could, to signifie that aspiration, that is for the ch, dh, th, and sh . So
will I doe the like for this lh, as thus, ɫ:
wherevnto the folowing letters may wel
ioyne, and the difference sufficient . Further, we abuse the name of h, calling it
ache, which sounde serueth very well to
expresse a headache, or some bone ache :
whose propertie is to signifie onely the
breath without any meane of instrument
or sound as we vse it before and after the
sound

(marginal handwritten notes:)

l aspirata: v.
I take it he is
deceued: for the
welsh ll is a
mere aspirat
like v th. or t.
& hath no voice.
but our l. in
able is fully
broken on the
arterie & is
ll vocall.

ɫ: I new.

h. ache:
H a mere guttu
rall, moueth neither
tongue nor lip.
It forceth, or thick
ens the breath
sometime before
sometime after
the vowell.

sound of the vowell in laughing hah, oʒ
heh, as when we laugh we bʒing out our
bʒeath so hah, hah, hah: oʒ heh, heh, heh,
where the h, hath no sounde but as you
woulde blowe to warme your handes, foʒ
the sound therof is shewed by the vowell.
And foʒ that we doe vse to wʒite so many
diuerse secretarie hands, amongst which,
there hath not yet one bene framed to be
put in pʒint, and seeing the Italick letters
much wʒitten and pʒinted amongst vs,
I do herafter vse them, and doe find them
as easie and swift foʒ the hande and eye,
as any other letter, howbeit there are
many in diuerse nations doe wʒite their
accustomed hande very swiftly, whereof
much vse is onely the cause, but none so
generall and thoʒowly easie foʒ the eye,
and hand, as the Italick. And foʒ the new
figures, which I haue deuised, confoʒma-
ble to the course of the hande, and fit foʒ
the pʒint, no man nædeth to be offended,
who so liketh them not, may leaue them.
Yet who can let me to think of him otherwise, than as of a man which liketh best
to be partly naked, and wilfully refuseth
conue-

conuenient and fit clothes to furnish the
want of his conuerture, and yet is content to haue some part touble o2 treble
furnished, with none other reason than
bicause he hath bene b2ought vp in it, and
is the vse of his countrie, whereas if the
superfluous attire were bestowed on that
other part which wanted, he should be no
mo2e burthened than befo2e. Euen so our
number of figures o2 letters shall be no
mo2e than befo2e , but shaped to better
purpose, leauing all superfluitie, and taking what næde is, as is partly sayd. Fo2
you may sæ (and you shall finde that wæ
nædethem not) I haue left the y, and w,
wholy. To the c, I haue giue an addition
fo2 ch . The j, consonant and q, I leaue
also as wholye superfluous . So are the
long s, and this figure 2, fo2 that one figure fo2 one sounde is sufficient, except
we would haue sto2e, as is vsed of men in
battell, o2 fo2 wiues when one husbande
is dead, another to dwell in the place: but
we sæ there nædeth no such supplye in
letters. Further, fo2 ŷ right placing of h,
I am not so much bounde to custome, but

s, 2, h ff.

Placing
of h.

L.j.   that

An Orthography.

that I may write it as we vſe it in ſpeach, as for theſe words, what, when & where,

H: præcedit vocalem.

I doe write, huat, huen and *huer*, and all ſuch like.

I leaue alſo all double conſonants: hauing a marke for the long bowell, there is therby ſufficient knowledge giuen that euerye vnmarked bowell is ſhort : yet wheras by cuſtome of double conſonants there may be doubt of the length, we may vſe the marke ouer it, of the acute tone or tune, thus

The acute tune ´

Alſo I finde it as reaſonable for vs to

di, p, p, leſt. vſe the abridgement of, for halfe, p for our by, and p for our for, as &, for and, or any other abridgement, wherein no letter of

&, or &. the ſillable is ſhewed, but ſæing &, or &, is ſo vniuerſally vſed, I leaue it as I find it, ſo doe I the x, for that it is in likewiſe

x vſed vniuerſally in counting for ten , but for voyce it maye be expreſſed with ks, which I will often vſe for it, ſæking to eſchue diuerſitie of figures. The like maye be ſayd of li. for pound, d. for peny, ob, for halfepenye, and q . for farthing , but in s. for ſhilling, is ſome reaſon, of which, what

whatſoeuer I write or ſay, I know euery
man will vſe as him beſt liketh. But for
my part in the former abridgements and
ſuch like, ſæing they varye from the of=
fice and right vſe of letters, I will write
the ſillables at length, except it be when I
would write by ciphring: but for the reſt
laſt mentioned, I will vſe them with the
multitude, and the more willing, for that
they ſerue in matter of numbring, and
naming of kindes of monye: wherewith
none commonly deale, other than ſuch as
are capable, quickly to learne the ſayd ac=
cuſtomed figures.

Accordingly will I ſet them in order,
with their names, and examples of their
ſoundes, whereof I begin to wryte in
the next Chapter, and ſo continue all the
reſt of this worke: wherewith although
that which is ſayde may ſatiſfie the bene=
uolent, yet the taſte of ſome other will be
ſo altered, as the reſt will be right loth=
ſome vnto them, and grieue them to lœke
thereon, by the ſtraungeneſſe therof: vn=
to which paine (ſæing pleaſure is paine=
ful vnto them) I do driue them if they wil
            L.ij.   vnder=

An Orthography.

vnderſtande the ſame , by the experience
wherof, ſome of them may peraduenture
finde ſuch ſauour as they maye chaunge
their mæde . And for that the figures and
ſoundes of the vowels are preſcribed,
here followeth a table of the conſonants
and breathes, with a declaration of their
proper vſe and ſounde by this our preſent
maner of writing , for ſuch doubtfull
wordes as are therein written in my following new maner.

Figures.	Names.	Sounded before and after vowels, as in the wordes here-vnder.
1 { b	bi	b'rds, bil, dab , krab . For bille, dabbe, Crabbe.
p	pi	pild, pig, pap, paper, for pigge, pappe,
2 { v	ev	ev'er, eva, hev, lev . For heaue, leaue.
f	ef	eftſun, eſekt, if, thif. For eftſone, effect, if, theeſe.
3 { g	ga	gaul, gam, leg, bag. For gall, game, legge, bagge.
k	ka	kan, kaG , bak, zak. For canne, catch, backe, iacke.

4 { ɉ ɉc ɉentɉ, ɉorɉ, saɉ, paɉ. For gentle, george, sage, page.

G Gc Geri, Giz, ſuch, much. For cherie, cheeſe, ſuch, much.   juɔ muɔ

5 { d di dik, did, gud, lad Eor dick, didde, good, ladde.

t ti tib, tit, ſit, kit. For tybbe, titte, ſytte, kitte.

6 { d ed eđer uidout or uiđin. For eyther without or within.

ꝧ eꝧ ꝧri, ꝧik and ꝧin. For three, thicke and thinne, and heꝧ haꞇ hiꞟ deꝧ. For beaꞇh, hath, his death.

7 { z ez ezi hoz. For eaſie hoſe.

ſ ſſ eſter, eſt-uind. For eaſter & eaſt winde, ſend mi ſum ſalt. For me ſomme.

{ l el }
{ m em } Whoſe ſounds are ſo vniuer-
{ n en } ſally kept perſite and ſimple as
{ r er } is ſayd as I neede to giue none example of them.

đ eđ Before the vowell we doe nɔt vſe it, but after, as bedđ, habđ, ſabđ. For beadle, bable, ſable.

ſ   aſ   aſ, aſes, ſal, ſi uaſ. For aſhes, ſhall ſhe waſhe.

h   bah,   bah, hch, and hath no ſounde but of the vowell.

Breathes two. { ſ / h }

(handwritten marginalia:)
p. b. g. ʒ. d. đ. ʒ. l. m. n. r. ɖ : ouant obhia : tanquam gemunt.
p. f. k. c. t. ɵ. s : n. 8.
expertes oni ono.
Spiritus duplex : { ſ / h }
8. ſpirat per dentes
h ſpirat libera e pectore. //////
Litera 26.
Vocales: 5.
Spiritus: 9.
Soni obtuſi: 12.

Thus I finde in our ſpeach, the firſt of ech of the .viij. paire, figured by *b, v, g, ʒ, d, đ,* and *ʒ,* with the foure liquides or ſemiuocales l, m, n, r, and the *ɖ* to haue the dull, dumb, inward or groning ſoundes of the breſt, and the latter of eche of the ſeuen paires neuer to be ſounded (but only breathed) otherwiſe then by the helpe of the vowell or ſemiuocale, and are p, f, k, c, t, ɵ, and s. And the two other aſpiratios or breathes, thone blowen thorow the teeth, and thother freely without any ſtop from the breſt: and are figured ſ, and h. ſo there are twelue dumb diuers ſounds, nine diuerſe breathes, and the fiue bowels, which make in all. xxvj. ¶ I finde not that we næde any moꝛe ſimple figures.

Of

Of, the accidentes vnto vowels, to
weete, time, tune, and breath, with
Diphthongs and Triphthongs,
and an order of diſtincti‐
on and pointing v‐
ſed thereafter.
Cap. vj.

modo vocalis fortiter
sonat ut thine : nus.
modo consona ut min.

N Owe for the quantitie of
ech of the bowels, which
is an accident to the boice,
to giue knowledge when
the bowell ſhall be longer
in the ſame ſounde, one
marke for that length may ſerue well for
all and euery one of them: for which as is
ſayd, I vſe a pricke vnder ech, as thus,
a e i o u. And when the following conſo‐
nant is to be harder ſounded than accuſto‐
med (for which we now vſe to double
them) the note of the acute vpon the pre‐
cæding bowell, may fitly ſerue as is ſayd
Folio 36 ¶ when two bowels may come
togither, and by the ſpeach are founde in
two ſillables, the figure of diuiſion called
Dyæreſis may ſerue well, as is ſayd, Fo‐
lio. 35. which I doe alſo vſe, and of the

sic pate. pat.
hide. hid.
main. man.
made. mad.
seat. set.

Vocalis longa
notatur puncto
infra subscripto.

Consona fortis,
notatur virgula.

+40

L.iiij.   breathes

Diphthongus: e geminis vocalibus.
e breui cum longa:

An Orthography.

3 8 e 3?

bꝛeathes, Folio 34. ꝉ 35. Now wil I ſhew
you examples of the Diphthongs made of
two ſhoꝛt vowels, and of others of one
ſhoꝛt and of another long. And then of
triphthongs. VVith ſhoꝛt vowels, as thus,

ui, ue, ui,
ei, ie, iu, ou.

(ui uil reid bei ionder uel, huer ðe uat uas
uelner takn bei ðe iung hound) which is
wꝛitten foꝛ (we wyll ride by yonder well
where the VV at was wel neare taken by
the yong hound) which doe come very often in our ſpeach.

Of diphthongs whereof one bowell is

ua, ue, iu,
ou.

ſhoꝛt, and the other long as (iu uer ua-
king in ðe fourts tour, huer az ðe bue did pour
uater upón ðe huet flour) which I wꝛite foꝛ
(you were waking in the folwerth tewer,
when as the boye did poure water vppon
the wheate flower) which alſo doe come

uei.
ieu.

berie often. And foꝛ triphtongs as (bi ueiz
ov ðe hueiz buei) foꝛ, be wiſe of the hoyes

uei.

bowy. And (hark ðe kat duth mieu hueiz iu
milk ðe ieu) foꝛ, hark the Cat doth mewe,

eau.

whiles you milke the yowe. And a Baſin
and eaur, foꝛ, eawer, and certaine others
as will be ſæne hereafter . And foꝛ thꝛæ
vowels comming togither, and making
                                                              two

two ſillables as in example (*de viuĕr ſeᵈ* | *iuë.*
ſiuĕr it iʒ puĕr) foʒ (the bewer ſayth ſure
it is pure) ¬ as in theſe woʒdes (*dis beiĕr iʒ* | *ciē, ouĕr.*
beiĕr oʒ pouĕr den de deiĕr bes biʒ ſeiĕr . Foʒ
this bier is higher of power, than the dier
by his fire .) And ſo of others when they
ſhall come in place hereafter, and foʒ the
Apoſtrophe ¬ coniunction of halfe woʒds, | *Apoſtro-*
oʒ of diuers woʒds which ſhall be ſounded | *phe.*
togither, their vſe is common. | *Coniunc-*
| *tion.*

At laſt, to be readye to enter into my
newe maner of wʒiting, I will brieflye
wʒite of diſtinction oʒ pointing , which
(well obſerued) maye yelde the matter,
much the readier to the ſenſes, as well to
the eie as to the eare . Foʒ it ſheweth vs
how to reſt: when þ ſentence continueth, | *suspend continuing*
and when it endeth : how to vnderſtande | *Rest*
what is wʒitten, and is not needefull to | *Ending concludē*
the ſentence : what ſome tranſlatour oʒ
new wʒiter of a woʒke, doth adde moʒe
than the Authoʒ did at firſt wʒite : and alſo what ſentence is aſking: and what is
wondʒing : their number is ſeuen, whoſe
figures folow. The firſt marked thus ,
the Greekes call comma , foʒ which the

Latins

An Orthography.

Latines and other vulgares haue vsed a strike thus / o₂ thus, / ¶ called it inci-sum, and is in reading the sho₂test rest, neare the time of a Crachet in musicke, alwayes signifying the sentence vnfini-shed which we commonly nowe marke thus , fo₂ that the vse thereof is so often to be seene, I fo₂beare to giue you any o-ther example therof.

Comma
,

Colon
:

The second marked thus : ỹ Greekes call colon, which the Latines interp₂ete artus membrorum o₂ internodium, which is the space, o₂ the bone, fleshe and skinne betwixt two ioyntes, and so (ac-compting a full sentence, as a complete bodie) these two p₂ickes may well signifie a great part therof,: as of the body, may be taken from the ancle ioint to the knee, and from the knee to the huckle o₂ buttock ioynt: and knowing thereby that there is mo₂e to come, whereas the other first rest o₂ comma, doth but in maner deuide the small parts (betwixt the ioynts) of the hands and feete.

Periode
thus
And the last of these th₂ee is a p₂icke thus   to signifie the ende of a full and per-

perfite sentence, as the head and feete are
the extreeme endes of a body, which prick
the Greekes and Latines with many o=
ther nations doe vse: and the sentence be=
fore it, they call Periodus that is in latine
circuitus vel ambitus, and after some
comprehentio, and we sentence, after
which we vse to begin with a great letter.
Anye one of the other foure markes, al=
though they may be for perfite sentences,
yet may they be put within other longer
sentences. As the Parentheseos, which
Greeke word signifieth interposition: and   ( )
we may vnderstand to be a putting in, or
an addition of some other matter by the
waye: which being left out yet the sen=
tence remayneth good. And note that it
may be put in any part of the sentence,
except it be at the beginning or ende: and
the sayd Parenthesis are most so short as
there doth seldome chaunce in it anye o=
ther of the three foresayde points. Some=
times the right halfe circle is vsed of the
tranflatour to signifie his expofition or
glose, vpon some worde or sentence, and
some doe vse both for that purpose: wher=

An Orthography.

by it is to be knowen to be the translators mynde, and not the Authors, and then they be not vsed for interposition of sentence: for which vse the two last herevnder are most vsed. The vse of the Parenthesis is so wel knowen as I neede to giue none example of it. No more doe I of the interrogatiue or admiratiue, but that they are most full sentences of themselues, & therefore are also marked with the full sentence, point or pricke in the line, adding therto for asking aboue ẏ line thus: & for wondring thus! And for the marke of the interrogatiue and admiratiue, I woulde thinke it more reasonable to vse them before then after, bicause their tunes doe differ from our other maner of pronunciation at the beginning of the sentence. Which I thought good to remember, but to vse them as they are receiued, seeing the matter is of no great moment. There resteth yet to saye somewhat of these last paire [ ] which differ from ẏ propietie of the Parenthesis: for it is neuer vsed of the Author, and first writer of any matter, but in translations, commentaries

Asking ?
wondring !

taries and expositions: in translations, as
is sayd aboue of the figures of interposit=
on, when as they haue no force of Parenthesis in expositions and commentaries,
contrarywise the writer noteth the text
(whether it be worde or sentence) some
with both, others with the right half, then
following he writeth his commentarie or
exposition. Thus to your twelue figures
for your diuers dumbe sounds and seauen
diuers breathed consonantes , and two
simple breathes, with your fiue vowels
ech short or sharpe, or long when it is so
sounded with the diphthongs and triph=
thongs which maye come of them, with
the other accents and distinctions or poin=
ting before particularly (though briefly)
declared : and vsing all accordingly, I
thinke euerye reasonable man (yea, I
mought say, childe or youth that can read
and doth vnderstand that which is before
said) may assuredly, without any occasion
of doubt , reade all that which followeth.

I woulde gladly haue had letters for
the capitals, greater & thicker than those
hereafter, alwayes of one sort & making,

M.iij.   for

for want wherof for this impreſſion I doe
vſe a ſtrike before them, which I haue
done for the yong and new learners be-
hoofe : for that I woulde not their eyes
ſhoulde be troubled with two figures
differing in ſhape, for anye one ſimple
voice, ſound, or breath, when as one may
ſuffice, and much leſſe for ſo many.

Now ſome ſuch as haue well conſide-
red the premiſſes maye thinke my meaning to be good, and yet can not be per-
ſwaded my purpoſe ſhould euer be ſo profitable as I haue promiſed in my preface,
for that the preſent maner is ſo plentiful-
ly ſpread, and that in great volumes, and
is vniuerſallye receyued, and well liked
of, as it ſhoulde be a maruailous labour
and charge to allowe a new maner. And
therefore it is the moſte profitable to be
contented with the olde. That is, ſaye I,
bicauſe no better nor more certaine order
hath bene hitherto laid before them. Theſe
men meane to be content with Acornes
as their predeceſſours were, contenting
themſelues with Hides and Felles for
their clothing, and Apernes to gather
their

their acornes in, and dwell in their dens, rather than to fell the wood, and make them houses therewith, to stocke vp the rootes and make the grounde arable, to plowe the grounde and sowe and reape good corne. And therefore I say, how long soeuer our predecessors haue vsed our present maner, when we do not receyue and enioy therby the benefite of a perfite writing, but contrarywise do finde great disorders in it, (as it hath appered) we should rather imbrace than repugne the better and more profitable, and be ashamed of our former rudenesse: for in amendment of any thing it is better late than neuer.

A.7.

An Orthography.

An exersiz ov dat huiG iz sed: huer-in iz de-
clard, hou de rest ov de consonants ar mad
bei dinstruments ov de mouts: huiG
uaz omited in de premisez, for dat
ui did not muG abiuz
dem. Cap. vij.

Pn dis titd abuv-uritn, ei konsider ov de j, in exersiz, & ov de
u, in instruments: de leik ov de
j, in titd, huiG de kómon man,
and mani lernd, du sound in de
diphthongs ei, and iu: ict ei
uld not think it mit to ureit dem, in doz
and leik urds, huer de sound ov de voël onli, me bi as uel dlouëd in our spiG, as dat ov
de diphthong iuzd ov de riud: and so far ei alou
observasion for derivasions. ∞ / hierbei iu me
persev, dat our singd sounding and ius of letters, me in proses ov teim, bring our hol nasion
tu on serten, perfet and zeneral speking. ∞
/ huer-in si must bi riuled bei de lernd from
teim tu teim. ∞ / and ei kan not blam ani man
tu think dis maner ov niu ureiting stranz, for
ei du konfes it iz stranz tu mei self, dob befor
ei

ei hav ended de ureiting, and iu de riding ov
diz buk, ei dout not bod' iu and ei Sal tink
our laburs uel bestoëd. ∞ / and not-uid-standing dat ei hav devizd dis niu maner ov ureiting for our /inglis, ei mien not dat /latin
Suld bi-uritn in dez leters , no mor den de
/grik or /hebriu, neder uld ei ureit t' ani
man ov ani Stranz nasion in dez leters , but
huen az ei-uld ureit /inglis. ∞ / and az ei-uld
gladli konterfet hiz Spic uid mei tung, so-uld
ei hiz ureiting uid mei hand. ∞ / iet huo kuld
let mi t'iuz mei pén de best ei kuld, derbei t'-
aten de super tu de perfet pronunsiasion, ov a-
ni Stranz Spic : but ureiting /inglis, ui me
(az is sed) iuz for evri Stranz urd , de sam
marks or leters ov de voises huic ui du seind in
Spic, uidout ani-uder regard tu Siy bei-ureiti-
ting huens de-urd iz boroëd , den az ui du-in
Speking. ∞ / for suc kuriozite in superfluz leters, for derivasion or diferens, and so furs, iz
de disordring and konfounding, ov ani-ureiti-
ting : kontrari tu de lau-ov de perfeksion der-
of, and agenst aul rezon : huer-bei, it Suld bi o-
bedient untu de pronunsiasion, az tu hir ladi
and miStres : and so, ád or diminiS az Si Saul
in sukses ov teim kómaund . ∞ / furder bi-iu

N.I.   adver-

adٞvertiƷed, ƌat ci me ofin iuƷ boƌ ƌe feluƷ ꝏr
siſters ꝏv ꝏn per, in ꝏn urd, at ꝏn teim d' ꝏn, and
at an-uƌer teim d' uƌer. ꝏ / aƷ for exãpƚ in ƌis
huiᴸ ei hav hier-befor uritn, in ƌis urd ius,
uid s, and hav uritn ƌe sam urd aulso, uid hir
felu Ʒ, so hav ci dun ui' d'artikƚ ꝏv and of.
for ƌat ui du-iuƷ ƌem so in spiᴸ. ꝏ / hier,
bei ƌekſampƚ ꝏv d' /hebriu dagheƷing and
rapheing, ꝏv six ꝏv ƌer konſonants, and pri-
king ꝏv ƌe riht ꝏr leſt ſeid ꝏv ƌer léter / sin,
iƷ noted ƌe dubƚ ius ꝏv our ſed 7. perƷ of felu konſonants, and ƌoƀ it bi not in ƌe ſam sort,
aƷ ci tak it : for our diferens iƷ tu kno huen
d' ꝏn haſ d' inuard sound and d' uƌer not: and
ƌerƷ, iƷ huen d' ꝏn iƷ harder breƌƌ ƌan d'-
uƌer, aƷ me bi from our b, and bh, if ui-iuƷd
it : ꝏv ƌe g, soft , and ƌe gh aſpird, aƷ ƌe
/ fleming duƌ iuƷ it : from our d, and dh, in
suᴸ-ueiƷ aƷ is ſed hier-after ꝏv ƌe ph: our and
ƌe / grik k, from ch. and χ. p, from ph, not
aƷ ui-and ƌe modern / griks du-in ƌe sound
ꝏv f, huiᴸ if ƌe bib / duᴸ had found gud, ƌe
kulƌ as uel hav iuƷd ph, aƷ pf, in pfund for our
poũd: but if ƌe had takn ƌe b, ƌe-uld hav breƌƌ
it in ƌis plas, as ƌe du-auluerƷ : huiᴸ iƷ aƷ ui
muht for pound in ƌis ueiƷ p-hound: so ƌe ureit
pfeiſſ for a flint or peip, huiᴸ if it had bin uritn
                   uid

uid ph, ŝe iuld haʋ soŭded it az muht bi p-heiff:
so for oepffel, œp-hel offen, op-hen : pſlaum,
p-hlaum: pfennig, p-hennig: in huiꝿ urds ui
in /ingliſ, having ſapt ſem uidout de ſ, or h,
iet ui breſ de h, softli and ſę: p-heip, ap-hel,
p-hluin, op-hen and p-hēni:oʋ de t, from th, az
ui-iuz th, in de river oʋ /thams, /thomas and
/sathan, az de /ualſ du-aluez iuz it : and
de /duꝿ in dez urds zŭm theil theŭr, thor and
thŭn, in /ingliſ sum del dičr, dor and dun :
huiꝿ, ar neʋer konfounded in de sound or
breſ oʋ eder d, or ts. ∞ dº /hebrius
for-sed daghes iz a prik in de bodi-oʋ de léter,
tu giʋ de knolez oʋ a harder, and raphe a litſ
lcin oʋr-it for de softer sound. ∞ /ei remember
dat sum oʋ our grámarians for de present
mihi, and nihil, did ureit michi and ni-
chil, and so sounded ch, in de sound oʋ ꝿ, az
ei aulso remember de /frenſ did in 8, huiꝿ
boſ ui, and ŝe haʋ uel left prezentlei. ∞ /and
huer-az de béter lerned sort baʋ iuzd ch, in
/michaelmas, az't-uer uritn uid kh, or k, alon,
az abuʋe: in mani plases oʋ /ingland de
kuntreman iz dkuſtumed tu sę for de quarter
de /miꝿelmas: and ict bi-nil kaul biz kom-
panion /mibel. ∞ /and so de /nordren man

sez mikl for our miꝧ or muꝧ, kirk for ꝧurꝧ,
and suꝧ leik. ∞ /hier-beï't-iz evident dat ui
abiuz de h,tu mak it serv so diverslei uid kon-
son.ints az ui du, huiꝧ (az iz bifor-sed ov de
voëls) ui-ar konstrend tu du, having no seve-
ral leters for doz konsonant sounds : huiꝧ ui-
iuz in our spiꝧ, huiꝧ sounds de /latins never had, nor de /duꝧ, nor /frens, nor d'
/italian. ∞ / for de /latin, from huom
de sed nasions uid vs, du bor' our leters.
Æneas Siluius *in his treatis* de liberorum
educatione, *ner de later end, writing* de
aspiratione *sets:* Apud Latinos nulla
consona aspiratur. /and a litl after hi
notet dat inⁿ . ar iuzd tu b'aspird in
/ grik uurds, to uit c,p,r,t, az Chremes,
Philosophus, Rhetor, and Thraso . and
uder derivasions ov de /grik: and duts aulso
der not, dat de /latins uer not skrupelus in ob-
serving ov derivasion, az mei kontrariez uld
hav us, az Filius, Fama, and Ferè, de hav
aluez uitn uid f, doh de bi derivd from de
/ grik. / de leik iz der in annotationes
Ioachimi Camerarij, Iohannis Si-
chardi, aliorumꝗ doctiſsimorum in
vtraꝗ lingua virorum: *upon* Quintili-

a 2

an, *in an impresiõ at* Basil *bei* Robert
Winter *in* Anno. 1543. *in de first buk in de
seivth Capter,* de literis & eorum potes-
tate, sub litera e. Et F, litera vtimur
pro aspirato: quæ enim Græci per φ,
enunciarunt, Latini per F, maluerũt:
vt fama, fagus, fur, afer. Quæ igitur
Græci inquit, aspirate pronunciarũt,
nos quidem non aspirate dicimùs, sed
tamen consimiliter. *∞ / d'understanding huerof me litl profit ani-user den de
/ grámarian, huerfor ei du not inglif it. ∞
/ and den folueth dis sentens:* Docuit enim
& Priscianus, inter F, & φ, proferen-
dum differentiam esse. &c. vt Burrhus
pro Pyrrho, Bruges pro Phrygibus,
Balæna pro Phalena. *∞ /huiG signifieth:
and* Priscian *triuli tauht, dat der iz a diferens in prouunsiasion betuikst f, and ph, and
so furth, az* Burrhus, *for* Pyrrho, Bruges
for de Phrygians, Balæna *for* Phalæ-
na. *∞ / and* Quintilian *resiteth der in de
text dat* Cicero *lauht ✕ on tu skorn in speking*
Fundanio, *for dat hi kuld not pronouns de
first leter ov d'urd az de. / latins did. ∞
/ huer-bei iu me persev d'aunsient /latins*

N 5.   *urat*

urat az ðe spak and understud ðe / griks as-
piring of p, tu bi ner leik az ui muht aspir
b, and ðerfor urat ðoz urds uid b, ðoh ðe
/ griks urat ðem uiþ ph. ∞/ for ðe riht sound
ov p, breðd, kan not bi diskreibd in / ingliſ
akustumed ureiting, for ðat ui-iuz ðe ſ, for ð
abiuzd sound ðerof, and kontrari-ueiz du
sound ph, in / grik urds in ðe sam sound ui-iuz
ð'f, huiſ dus ápir (bei ðat is sed) oht not tu
bi so sounded : but breðd az in ðe / duſ examples befor ∞/ and ðoh ei hav ſeuëd in hier-
befor hou-ui du-iuz ðe t, breðd in / thams,
/ thomas, and / sathan, iet ei-uil se som-huat
mor ðerof in dis plas, ðe / latins in translating
ov / grik urds for ðer ius, hav put θ intu boð
t, and d, as θριάμβος triumhphus, θεος
deus, θεα dea : but du-iuz th, az in The-
ma, Thesis, Thermopola, and mani-uðer
suſ urds az ðe bor' ov ðe / griks. ∞/ and ui-
iuz tu breð it riht also-in ðez urds of thuni-
fis, herb theim, medesin thriaks, threziur and
thron, in huiſ az in ðe abuv-sed / thams,
/ thomas, and / sathan, ui-iuz it az du-aul
/ duſland over and neðer, and az du ð' / italian, / frenſ, and / spaniard, non ov ðem hauing ðoz sounds in aul ðer spiſes huiſ ui
                                        hav

hav givn tu th, nor never had de /latins dem,
derfor hou kuld ui-urcit dem ui' de /latin
leters, iet our predesesors abiuzd de d, in ad,
and aul de kompounds derof, in de sound ov d,
eksept d'urd huer-uid it iz kompounded began
uid d, az dico, and duco, in suG de foloing
d, did konstren dem tu sound de former riht.∞
/and mor hav ui abiuzd de t, in de sound ov
ti, in de tird persons singuler ov aul verbs ak-
tivz and neuters ending in t, uid a voel befor it : and for d, in apud, de t, in caput,
&c. az iz plenli sed in d'orthographi ov de
gramer, huiG not-uid-standing ci ser mi, sum
of mein elders biing broht up d'erin-uil tink de
kan not spek beter nou'den de did huen de-uer
iung, espesiälei dat huiG de lernd in de
gramer skul : but buat! iu metink ci-am nou
forti ov mei mater, tu-urcit ov speking, huer-as
ci purpozd but tu sio hou-ui muht most fitli
urcit dat ting ui spek! so ci du, doh ci-urcit hier
ov d'il speking ov /latin, in suG ov our /ing-
liß sounds az de /latins nor no nasion els (tu
mei knolcz) but de /ualß (from huom it must
nids bi, our predesesors hav lernd dem) and
our /ingliß /gresians du-iuz. ∞ / nou for
de breding ov c, (for huiG ci iuz G) ui abiuz
N.4.   muG,

muȝ, but haȝ iuȝd riȝtli-oftn aȝ in de nams
oȝ Cham , Chanahan , Chryſoſtom,
Charybdis, *and in deȝ urds, chronikd, chant
ov a kuntre, choler, a karnaȝ chart, a chandd, a
chanel, de herb sichore, and mani-uder, and aȝ
aul Duȝ-land, and de /florenteins du-iuȝ it
auluȝ.∽ /huiȝ sound oȝ ȝ, de /italian and
bib /duȝ and /spaniard haȝ, aȝ is sed, and
ȝaul-bi in de nexȝt ȝapter : but de /frenȝ in
mani urds huer-in d'oriȝinal /latin iȝ uritn
uiȝ c, de ureit ch, sounding it aȝ our sh, huer-aȝ
ui du kip de sound ch, aȝ ei haȝ aluȝ-sed, or of
k, aȝ* Campus *ui se kamp , and de /frenȝ,
ȝaump :* Cattus, *a kat, ung ȝat :* Caules,
koluȝts, in /frenȝ shoulx : Capus, *a kapn,
shappon :* Carbo, *kol, sharbon :* Caſtellum,
kasɪd, shateau : Caldarium , *a kauderon or
kétd, sh.audiere∽ /iet oȝ laȝt sum oȝ dem haȝ
espeid d'éror , and haȝ deveiȝd tu boro de
spaniȝ c, uid an s, vnder, dus ç. and oftn, ui
ɪ:aȝ turnd de /latin c, intu de sound oȝ ȝ, aȝ*
Caſtus, *ȝast :* caſtigatio, *ȝastiȝing, ca-
ſeus, ȝiȝ :* capitulum, *ȝapter :* cantor,
a ȝaunter : cantio , *an inȝauntment :*
cancellarius, *a ȝauncelour :* cambio , *ei
ȝanȝ :* capella , *a ȝápel :* camerarius , *a*
ȝam-

Gamberlain: cerasus, a Geri ꝑ cerasum,
a Geri: cathedra, a Ger: huiG de / frenG
turn intu sh, as de rest: ckṣept it bi for Gi z,
huich de hav not derivd from / Latin, but kaul
it / formaȝe ∞ / and hier iz tu bi noted, bei
huat rezon ui se-and wreit, kart, karter, kamel,
and kandel, and iet wrds derivd from dem, ui-
alter intu de sound of G, az in Garrot, Gar-ked,
Gamlet and Gaundler: huer-in mi think, uer
sum profit tu kip de sound ov der primitivs,
sijng d etimologi ov de wrd muht de beter bi
knon der-bei, if derivasion uer so nedful tu li
kept az sum du think. ∞ / and for dat de komon
ius iz tu-wreit, kart, kandd, kamel and karter
uiṭ k, or c, uidout de h, ei me turn der oun en-
zin agenst dem-selvs, and feind faut in dat de
wreit not az d'orizinal wrds ar, tu giv mi knolez
huens de wrd iz derivd. ∞ / and dat muht de
uel du if de c, uer aspird, az is sed in Cham,
Chanahan, and choler &c. / huiG iz noting ner de sound ov our most komon alius ov
ch, huer-for ei hav deveizd G ∞ / dus ei trust
iu-under-stand sufisientlei hou rezonabd it iz,
tu-iuz de léter ov de breṭ h, onli befor and after
voelz and suG sounds az ar mad onli-ov dem ꞉
and for de komoditi huiG (bei dis teim iu me

O. I.   51)

si) ꝺꝛ mę kum tu de living oꝛ our nasion *and
our posteriti*, bei reseȝing oꝛ so mani léters aȝ
uꝛ-iuȝ voises, sounds or breds and iuȝing dem
auluȝ in der proper and pekulier ófises, *iu uil
not bi so muG ófended at dis invension, aȝ per-
aduentiur iu uer at first oꝑening oꝛ ꝺe buk*. ∞
/ and for mei leving oꝛ serten léters huer-of ui
had.ij.Saps for on sound, aȝ dis ȝ,& long ſ, and
oftn x,ui si hueder ui bi súſisiētlei servd uidout
dem or not. ∞ / huiG exsés oꝛ sum léters, *and
uant oꝛ uders,* Priſcian *noted in ureting oꝛ ꝺe
aksidents oꝛ leters, huer hi sēꝥ*, Authoritas
quoꝗ tam Varronis quam Macri, teſte
Cenſorino, nec k, nec q, neꝗ h, in nu-
mero adhibet literarū. Videntur tamē
& i, u, cum in conſonantes tranſeunt,
quātū ad poteſtaté, quod maximū eſt
in elemētis, aliæ literæ eſſe præter ſu-
pradiĉtas. Multum enim intereſt, u-
trum vocales ſint an conſonantes: ſicut enim, qnamuis in varia figura, &
vario nomine ſint k, & q, & C, tamen
quia unam vim habent tam in metro,
quam in ſono, pro una litera accipi
debent: ſic i, & u, quamuis unum nomen & unam habent figuram, tam
uoca-

An Orthography.

vocales quam consonantes , tamen
quia diuersum sonum , & diuersam
vim habent in metris, & in pronunti-
one syllabarum, non sint in eisdem
(meo iudicio) elements accipiendæ. ∾
/ and so hi prosideth ʃeuïng ᴆe diferens betuixt
ᴆe voël and ᴆe konsonant. ∾ / huer-bei iu me
si, hi (nor ᴆoȝ autours beʃor him) did ᴂkount
noᴆer k, nor q, nor h, in ᴆe number ov ᴆe / latin
alphabet, and deklard plenli ᴆat huen i, and u,
uer mad konsonants ᴆe simd tu bi-uᴆer léters,
(touᴅing ᴆer pouërs, huiᴅ iȝ ᴆe ᴅifest in elements) ᴆen ᴆ'abuv-sed, tu uʃt ᴆen voëls. ∾
/ and kompars ᴆat leik aȝ k, q, and c, hav divers ʃaps and nams, and hav but on pouër, aȝ
uel in miter aȝ in sound, and derfor oht tu bi
takn for on léter : so i, and u, doh ᴆe hav on
nam and on figiur; as-uel being voëlȝ aȝ konsonants, iet bikauȝ ᴆe hav deivers sounds and
deivers pouërs, bod in miters and in pronunsiasion of silabᴅs, ᴆe bi not (bei his opinion) tu bi
takn for ᴆe self and sam elements ∾ / ov huiᴅ
opinion uaȝ aulso Claudius Cæʃar, ᴆempe-
rour, huo hueilst hi uaȝ a private man, found
uant ov léters, for ᴆe / latin ureiting, and ᴆen
mad a treatiȝ, huer-in hi ʃcuëd ᴆe reȝons hou

O.2.   mit

mit it uas, tu·iuz tri-uder leters fit for de
voises spokn : huiG hi found tu bi for de v, konsonant de Aeolian / grik gáma dubled on
abov duser leik de / romain kapital F, but
turned dounward dus ꟻ, huiG hnen hi kam tu
bi / emperour, uas muG iuzd bod in / rom,
and els-huer, bu· de knolez derof kam untu but
a feu in respect ov de multitiua, huer-for it tuk
non efekt after him. ∞ / d'ius derof uas ment
tu hav kept de u, auiuas voël (az ei du in dis
treatis, and urat Sergus and ꟻixit for Ser-
vus and vixit, and de / iota an-uder to put
a difrens betuixt de i, voël and konsonant, huiG
in si Priscian seindes rezonabl : and de dird
uas ꟻ, for huiG de / Latins found der ij leters
bs, or ps, az gud. ∞ / iu me rid der-of in de .xij.
buk ov Cornelius Tacitus, aulso C. Sue-
tonius and A.C. Sabellitus du-ureit der-
of. ∞ / huiG aulso de / grámarians and / ora-
tors, Papirian , Priscian and Quintilian hav remembred in treating ov léters . ∞
Æneas Silvius at dend ov de sekond presept
of hiz / rhetorik seti de / grik x, uaz found bei
on Karment in de teim ov Octavian , mad
leik a krós, signifeïnz de misteri ov de krusifeï-
ing ov / khrist tu kum : huiG hi menes tu bi
borouëd

borouëd ov de / griks, and put t'-an-uder
ius den ever de did, huiG uaz from de sound ov
our kh, tu gs, ks, or cs, huiG de iuzd befor, and
in me feind it rezonabl Suld bi so sil, for mé-
ter ov vois, but for numbring iu me iuz de x, az
most fit and kómodious der-untu. ∞ / and fier-
der in de sam presept hi seti aulso, dat z, uaz
but niuli found, and dat de /latins uer unt tu
urcit de dubl s, derfor : but de sound derof is
béter expréss uid ds, huiG mi d'inks had bin
mor fit dan de ss . ∞ de / grik, in old teims
did iuz der H, cut in .ij. dus ⱶ ꟸ (az de du
iet uiti der gret léters(d'on tu signifei der aspiration /dascis, and d'uder der / psile, huiG
de /latins hav takn huol for d'er breti and so
hav ui-and uder nasions from dem. ∞ /histo-
ri-ureiters du deklar dat léters uer not inven-
ted aul at ons, nor bei on man, but in divers a-
zes. ∞ / dus in leving ov old or taking of niu
léters ui must bi riuled bei de multitiud ov de
létred, huiG kan iuz ov de rezone-kómodite tu
bi had bei d'on, or diskómodite bei d'uder. ∞
/ and for kustum ov ureiting az ui feind it ov
our for-faders : for dat our predesésours uer never bound tu de leik, no mor ar ui at dis pre-
zent. ∞ / ei tak Quintilian for mein autor

(huo

(huo uid mani uders) dud deklar, in his sed
first buk treating ov orthographi, hou léters hav
from teim tu teim bin Ganȝd on in de plas ov
an-uder, and so bei reȝon, and for gud sound,
ar kontinued : aȝ namlei for vortices and
vorſius(uid uders in de sam maner (bi seþ
Scipio d' African did first Gaunȝ de o, in
tu e.∞ / and dat de skulmasters ov hiȝ deȝ
uret ceruom and seruom, uid u and o, bi
kaus de o, kuld not ȝiuin and bi konfounded in
on sound uiþ de u, voël, huiG nou iȝ uritn uid
an u, dubled,iet bei neder ov dem uaȝ de sound
ov de spiG deklard. ∞ / as mani lerned men
els du , so duþ aulso Æneas Silvius veri
larȝli déklar de Gaung ov léters from de radi-
kaul or first urd, tu de diuers ues in maner and
teim huerin it me bi spokn, ákording to de best
and most perfet spiG iuȝd, aȝ iu me ſi in hiȝ
treatiȝ,de liberorum educatione, in de
titds, Quomodo consonantes gemi-
nari poſſunt, & literæ mutari, and de
neȝst after, Quomodo varientur literæ. &c.∞

/ dus muG hav ei sed ov de kustum of
ureiting,bikaus sum lernd men in printing of
Quintilians urks, hav Gaungd a urd, making

*king de sentens klin agenst d'autors meind:
and derfor t'ópoz dem, and to kauz de kóreksi-
on der-of de best ei me, in his sentens sei-
ted in de. 9. lef ov diz buk, ei hav put* Non
quod consuetudo, *and dat to giv suG kó-
rupters ov ami manz sens a uarning ov der é-
rour.∞* Quintilian *treating de next Gapter
besor ov kustum:* Superest igitur consuetudo. &c. ∞ */huer hi seti it uer a máter tu
bi laubt at, t'dfekt de old spiG mor den dat iz
spokn, and derfor it iz nesésari tu kno huat ui
Saul kaul kustum: dat if it Suld tak nam ov
dat de most du, it Suld bi a most daunzerous
presept, not onli for de maner ov spiG, but (dat
huiG iz greter(ov leif.∞/ huens Saul dat ble-
sing kum, dat triu and gud tings Saul plez
mani? de vcises huiG me bi iuzd ov de multitiud, Saul bi no kustum, but in speking, ui kno
de unexpert vulgar du spek riudlei.∞ / derfor ei uil kaul kustum ov spiG, de konsent ov de
lerned, az ov living de konsent ov gud men.∞
/den in his sed Gapter ov orthographi.* Verũ
orthographia quoᴥ consuetudini seruit, ideoᴥ sæpe mutata est. Nam illa
vetustisssima transeo tempora, quibus
& pauciores literæ, nec similes his no-
stris

ſtris earum formę fuerunt,& uis quotþ
diuerſa ſicut apud Græcos.&c . *and a*
litd aftcr De mutatione etiam literarum, de qua ſupra dixi,nihil repetere
hic neceſſe eſt . Fortaſſe ſicut ſcribe-
bant, etiam ita loquebantur. ꝏ/ *hier-*
bei it duts dpir dat ei hav iuʒd de forſed,non,
tu bring de ſentens tu Quintilians *meaning,*
from dat de firſt korekter, ei Suld ſę korupter,
and uders after him, hav put in niſi *in deivers*
prints, under-ſanding dat hi had ment ov de
kuſtum ov ureiting , framing de ſentens dat
Quintilian *Suld bi kontented tu hi ſubiekt*
tu de kuſtom ov ureiting, and derfor tu-iuʒ it
ſo-aʒ hi found it, bueraʒ iu mę ſi bei dat is a-
buʒ-ſed, and bei-and dereſt ov hiʒ forſed ſen-
tens,dat hiʒ mening uas ov de kuſtum ov ſpiG
ꝯ akordingli,ei feind: Ego vero quod. &c
aʒ huo ſu liſt mę ſi in /polʒ /GurG-iard at de
ſein ov de braʒn /ſerpent-iiŋ,kopies ov do'n and
as mani ov d'uder ſort.ꝏ/ but t'eʒ and ſatis-
fei ſuG aʒ eſer uil not tak de pen , or for dis-
tans ov plas kan not komodiuʒ'ei, ei hav noted
hierafter de plaſes,de teims, and printers nams.
At Paris,Anno.1516. ex officina Io-
doci Badij aſcencij. /*aulso der* ,1527.
Nicho-

An Orthography.

Nicholai Sauatier. /at Bazil.1528. Io‑
anni Soter. /and *der*.1549. Roberti
Winter, *in huiꝯ. iiij. kopies it iꞎ* Ego vero
quod.&c. /*and at* Colein. 1541. Io‑
annis Gimnici. /at Paris. 1562. Ste‑
phani./ *at* Antuerp. 1548. Iohannis
Loeï. /*at* Bazil.1561. Nicholaï Bri‑
ling, *iꞎ printed* Ego nisi quod. *ꝯc* ∞
/*huꝯ láꞇer sort de kórektor ov de first kopi,
understud ꝺat* Quintilian (*bikauꞎ it is writn
in de Ꞓapter ov orthographi*) *ment it tu bi* con‑
suetudo scriptionis, *or uld fors us sꝛ t'un‑
derstand him, and found ꝺat* nisi *uld fram
beter for ꝺat purpꝍ : but bei ꝺat iꞎ sed it ꝺuꞇ
plenli dpir ꝺat hi ment as ꝺoh hi had writn at
lengꞇh.* Ego vero quod consuetudo ser‑
monis obtinuerit : sic. &c. /*aꞎ de rest ov
de sentens duꞇ꞉ giv, and aꞎ huo sꝛ duꞇ꞉ rid his
former Ꞓapter* De consuetudine, *and duꞇ꞉
konsider de diskurs ov hiꞎ orthographi huerin iꞎ
writn de sentens abuv-sed,* Verum ortho‑
graphia quoꝗ꞉consuetudini seruit , i‑
deoꝗ꞉ sæpe mutata est : *must he forsed tu
konfés ꝺat hi ment ov de kustum ov spiꝯ.* ∞
/*huer-for tu ꝺat maintener ov kustum and
his adherents, huer-bei our ureiting muht kon‑*

tiniu

f. 42

tiniu-in disorder, ei tioht it gud at ŏe begining
ov ŏiʒ buk, tu giv ŏem t'understand Quintilians *meaning, and derfor ura* non quod
consuetudo obtinuerit. /*and du biliv*
ŏat if Quintilian *had fobt ŏat ani mā Suld*
ever hav understud him so, hi-uld hav áded ŏat
ur d sermonis, *aʒ abuv, tu hav put ŏe máter*
out ov aul dout, aʒ hi duŏ at d'end ov his Gap-
ter De consuetudine, *seing*, Ergo con-
suetudinem sermonis, vocabo consen-
sum eruditorum, sicut viuendi, con-
sensum bonorum. ∞ / *ov hueʒ meind*
uaʒ aulso Æneas Siluius, *huo treating* De
liberorum educatione, *at d'end under*
ŏe titŏ Quomodo varientur literæ,
duŏ aulso seit in maner Quintilians *urds:*
and huo douteŏ ŏer autoriiiʒ, ŏer neizdum,
and gret lerning: bjing so-uniuersáli knon e-
mongst aul lernd men. ∞ /*and if iu resev ani*
friut ov ŏis mei labur, it iʒ but a krop gótn af-
ter ŏer invension, and espesiaulei of Quintilians, *ov hueʒ urks not-uiŏ-standing (aʒ iu*
me si bei mei steil and riud maner ov urciting)
ei never studied, uŏer ŏen touGing hiʒ seingʒ
for ŏiʒ máter: huiG is kontend in hiʒ first buk
hueer is uritn, Nemo tamen reperitur,
qui

qui fit ſtudio nihil conſecutus. ∞ / iet
haſ not mei hed bin trubled uiɗ muG ſtudi-in
aul mei leif, neverɗeles ei-uiɗ aul mei hart du
luv and honor suG aᵹ are lernd and vertiuᵹ. ∞
/ for iu me ſi bei ɗiᵹ litɭ treatiᵹ ei hav bin a
traveler hi-iond ɗe seas, emong vulgar tungs,
ov huiG, ɗat smaul knoleᵹ ei hav, haſ bin ɗe
kauᵹ ov ɗis mein enterpreiᵹ: and ɗer-uiɗ aulso
ɗe sight ov a treasiᵹ set furth in print at Paris, Anno. 1545. bei an uᵹɗi man uel
lerned boɗ in / grik and / latin namd **Leuïs**
Meigret ov **Lyon**, touGing ɗ'abius ov ɗe
ureiting ov ɗe / frenƷ tung, huoᵹ reᵹons, and
arguments ei du hier-befor partlei-iuᵹ, aᵹ hi
did **Quintilians** huom it ɗpird hi had uel
ſtudied. ∞ / and ei hav ſin deiuers / frenƷ buks
put furſ in print in ɗat his maner ov orthographi, ov sum uel likt of, and reſeᵹd, and ov u-
derᵹ left and repugned. ∞ / but huat gud and
notabɭ ſ‌ing kan tak a spidi rut, emongst a
multitiud, ekſept ɗe / prinſes and / guvernurᵹ
(bei ɗe graſ huiG / god me giv ɗem) du ſavor
and sum-huat kountenans it . ∞ / iet as seſ
Quintilian in his firſt Gapter ov his firſt
búk: præcipienda ſunt optima : quæ
ſi quis grauabitur, non rationi defue-

P.2.   rit,

rit,ſed homini. ∞ / huiϲ ſigmſcieħ , de
beſt ħings ar tu bi taught: uid huiϲ iv ani
man bi-ófended , de-uant ſuld not bi-in de
rezon,but in de man.∞ /and d'argument or
diʒ má·er biing dus far advanſed, ei dout not
but it uil-bi bei ſuvn ſekund Quintilians
favored,perſeited, frámd and iuʒd ſo, aʒ it me
bi for de kó·non uelħ: aʒ de teim ſaul kounſel
dem ∞

/ and nou ei hav ħoħt it oudtu ſio-iu,hou-iu
me uid de firſt ov eϲ per ov our felo konſonants
(iuʒing priks in dem huen de ſuld hav d'in-
uard ſoud,& leving dem unprikt huen de ſuld
uant it) ureit ani ħing in / ingliſ aʒ perſetlei
aʒ urħ d'·uder ſevn uiħ dem. ∞ / d'experiëns
huerof, ei lev tu ſuϲ aʒ d'underſtand mi, huen
and aʒ it me p'eʒ dem, and am kontented t'iuʒ
dem tugeder uiħ der ſeluʒ aʒ is ſed,doh de du-
inkes our number bei ſevn. ∞/houb' it, ſiing
de hav bin ſo-alouëd and iuʒd, ei ſik not tu go
bak tu de /hebriu maner agen in d'at point. ∞
/but for d'·ius of priks, for de kuantiti ov our
voë'ʒ, it duħ ſum-huat dliud tu de /hebriu
maner tu de-ei, but noħing in ſens: for d'iuʒ
der priks and litd ſtriks under der konſonants
for de divers ſounds of der voëls, and ui but for
de

ðe kuantitie of teim ov ours : and ðat after ðe
maner ov ðe /griks az is sed. ∾ / and uder-
ueiz, iu me-ureit veri briſli after ð° /hebriu
maner uiðout ani priks, under our konsonants,
for soūd ov ani voël, or ðe ſap ov ani-ov ðem, at
ani teim, ekſept it bi huē on or moɉ bi-uritn for
a huol silabð, uiðout ðe help ov ani konsonant
or breθ, az in ðez prónounɉ ei, ui, iu, & i, huer
at lest ðe láter must niðs bi-uritn tu giv
understanding of sum person and number : and
iet uiθ sum ákuentans of ðe máner and máter,
a man me bi-abð tu rid it perſetli, az huo-so
list me (bei ðe ue-ov pásteim) pruv. ∾ / ðis
kɉind ov ureiting uld bi dark, and sim in maner a ſeiſring : and iet bi ðat ſuld iuɉ it, eðer
for his oun remembrans, or exerſiɉing ðe sam
(uiθ sum man ov experiens biing mad privi
ðer-untu) bei miſeiv léters : ei biliv ðe ſuld
sufsientlei understand eↄ uder, for aul kómon máter, exsepting onli ðe nams of θings
proper and ápe'lativ : huerin a man muht er, if
ðe uer not uritn at lengθ. ∾ / ei du si no kómo-
diti in ð°ius ðerof : but haɉ ſcuëd iu, huat a
man me du if hi so pleɉ.

/ei haɉ uritn hier-befor ðat ei - uld ſeu-iu
in ðis niu máner ov ureiting, hou-eueri-on ov

P.3. our

An Orthography.

our sounds & breds, is mad uiti d'instruments
ov de mouti, az ei hav dun der, ov de feiv voëls, and ov z, s, 8, and f. ∞ / ei noted der, dat
de /frenk du-iuz de j, konsonant in a sound
huik ui-iuz not in our spik : huerof dis 8, ser-
veti for de sister der-of, uid us, az de ch, duti
uiti dem, having no-inuard sound, and ar bod
framd uiti kiping ov de tung from de palet and
bringing de titi tugeder, or d'on or uder lip tu
his kounter titi, and tirusting de breti tiru dem
uiti d'in-uard sound, for de /frenk j, konsonant : huik if uihad in ius, 8uld mak us de
aehtti per. ∞ / for uant huer-of de 8, duti re-
men tu-us, a breti uidout selu, huik d'-uder
vij. pers hav. ∞ / but for uant ov dat sound, ui
hav .iiij. uders huik de /frenk never iuz, tu
uit ov z, k, and d, ti, huik ar veri hard for
ani natural /frenk tu pronouns : uder dan suk
az ar brouht up emongst vs sum-huat in iuti. ∞
/ nou for dis per b, and p, de-ar mad uiti klos
b. lips : de first uiti d'in-uard sound, and d'-uder
p. uid-out ani sound, but opening de lips uiti
tirusting furti ov de breti, and neder maketi
ani vois but brei de help ov sum on or mor ov de
voëls. ∞ / de leik ov v, and f, huik ar mad bei
puting ov eder lip tu his kounter titi, tirusting
furti

An Orthography.

furﬆ de breﬄ for bod, for de first uiﬄ d'in-uard   v.
sound, and for d'-uder non: bod perʒ biing   f.
mad uidout stiring ov de tung t'-ani part ov
de tiﬄ or palet.∞ / de g, and k, ar mad bei púting ov d'iner part ov de tung tu d'uper gret   g.
tiﬄ or gumʒ, de first uiﬄ d'in-uard sound and   k.
d'uder uiﬄ de breﬄ onli. ∞ / de d, and t, bei
lęing ov iur tung ful in de palet ov iur mouﬄ,   d.
and tuɢing hardest ov iur for-tiﬄ, for de first   t.
uid d' in uard sound, and for d'uder non:
huiɢ tu last perʒ hav a serten stę ov de breﬄ
leik aʒ had de first per, huiɢ kauʒeﬄ it at de
seperating ov de parts, tu-uit ov de lips, and ov
de tung from de tiﬄ, tu bi de harder ﬅrust
furﬄ.∞ / de leik ov ʒ, and ɢ, bei púting de tung
tu de palet and for-tiﬄ softli, so aʒ de breﬄ bi   ʒ.
ﬅęd: for de first uid an in-uard sound, and for   ɢ.
d'uder non. ∞ / but de v, and f, and d'uder
tu perʒ hier-after hav a kontiniual uniform
breﬄ.∞ / for d, and ﬅ, bei púting ov de for part   d.
ov de tung, tu d'uper fortiﬄ: so softli aʒ de   ﬅ.
breﬄ mę pas uiﬄ de sound for d'on, and uidout
for d'uder, and for aul de rest der iʒ sufisientli
sęd, touɢing hou dę ar mad bei d'nistruments
of spiɢ.∞ / nou-ei trust iu-ar satisfeid touɢing de severaul léters for de pertikuler voïses
  ov

An Orthography.

ov our spi(c), uiᵗ severaul leters for everi-on ov
dem : and bei der ius hier-bifor, ei tᵬink iu
feind ᵭe maner ᵭer-of mor rezonabᵭ ᵭanour
former.∞/ huerfor tu gro tuards an end, ei-uil
brieᵮli ᵬeu-iu huat furᵭer belongs tu-a gud and
perfet ureiting.

/ sum, ar ov d'ᵬinion, ᵭat it bekums not an
/emprour, /priᵬs, or /nobᵭ man tu-ureit uel
aᵭ triuli : verelei,it is a persuazion ᵭat ᵭe na-
tiur ov man iᵌ mor redi t'obe- untu, and tu
liv eidᵭlei, or in sum uᵭer pleᵌant exersiᵌeᵌ ov
ᵭe bodi,raᵭer ᵭen ov ᵭe meind, but suᵬ parents
aᵌ uil-bi so persuaded, never tasted ov ᵭe suit-
nes ov learning. for sertenlei ᵭer uaᵌ never gret
lerned nor exseling man but kuld ureit uel and
triulei : ei dᵬount not uel on'li-in a sloᵬful ku-
riuᵌ pented ureiting , but ᵭe mor uniformlei
and strehter ani man duᵗᵬ ureit, no man douteᵗᵬ
but it iᵌ ᵭe beter : and ᵭat is never or seldum
obtend exept it bi bigun in iuᵗᵬ (aᵌ Quintilian seᵭ at larᵌ, in his seᵭ first buk) and konti-
niued ᵭer-uiᵗᵬ for a nobᵭ man uiᵭ mani-uᵭer
vertiuᵌ ivn from ᵭe nurs.∞/ and aulso uiᵗᵬ
ᵭe ᵬois ov ᵭe /nurs : and in ᵭe rest ov his seᵭ
institusions, tu hav lerned and vertiuᵌ tiutors
for ᵭexersiᵌ ov bod ᵭe tung tu spek and hand tu
ureit

ureit in aul vertiu-and gud liuing.∞ / and d̯at
me bi kauld a-uel urciting huen de ḥand is so
redi az in taking no kar, for de fẹr, uniform and
streht urciting, de meind me be huilei givn and
okupeiẹd upon de máter tu bi-uritn , uid
sum kar, d̯at it me bi lezibl az uel for ud̯rs, as
for de ureiter.∞ / and for triu-urciting, befor
der kan bi-ani perfet and sufisient riu'z givn
der-of, de parts ov spiG must bi konsidered,
huiG never ani man koula begin tu fram upon
ani siur ground, until de foundasion uer found
serten and gud: huiG non biing ḥer-befor
touGt de rest me bi dun de beter hier-after.∞ / and Saulbe füd a t̯ank-ful urk, az-uel
for de behuf ov our brod speking / ingliS, az d̯ẹ
/ ualS, / iriS, and / skótiS nasions, tu giv dem
t'understand de best spiG iuzd ov de lerned:
az aulso for aul ud̯er (ov huat-so-ever strang
nasion) huiG me dezeir tu kno de perfet sound
and spiG ov d̯ẹ / ingliS tung.∞ / ana for d̯ẹ ad-
vaunsment ov ḥim huiG Saul tak it in hand, ei-
uil briefli urcit huat ei feind (bei d̯at ei ḥav
hier-befor uritn) touGing our ius ov our seyn
pers ov leters in spiG . ∞ / and derfor ci-u'd
gladli-it had bin t̯rulei observd, but ov kurte-
zi ber uid mi, for d̯at iz past, ei-uil indeuor t'a-
mind

Q 1.

mend de soluing, de best ei me ∽

/ for dis urd ius, for hui G ui hav writn **vse,**
ui kuld hier-befor nev r feind diferens in ureiting, betuixt de / noun and de / verb, but wat
indiffentlei, **the vse is good, and I do vse
otherwise** (hui G sentens in gud suts ei-uaz not
redi tu-ureit, no mor ei tink uer iu tu rid)
buvraz ei feind our spi G iuzets in aul teims and
maners, (hui G de / latin grámarian kaulets
/ tenses and / modes) ov de urd uid, z, as ei-iuz,
dou-iuzest, hi-iuzets, ui, i, and de-iuz, iuzd,
iuzing & ∽ / & ov de nam uid aul prepofisi-
ons & artikels singulerlei uid s, but not plurali,
bikauz de konsonant kumets betuixt . ij . voëls,
buer-for it is turned intu z. ∽ / and furder ei
feind de z. iuzd in iz, az, hiz, diz, and su G
leik oftn, and dat akording tu de spi G, hui G
iet buen de soluing urd begimets uid s, d'order
ov de tung duts G aunz intu s, dus : iz uel, az
ani, hiz on, diz ue, but de soluing urd begining
uid s, or s, dus, is sed, as sun, his seing, dis
salt, and as s i, is samfast, his sert, dis sor.∽
/ hier iz tu bi noted dat de first ov d'uder bre-
ded tu per of konsonants, tu-uit v, and d, me
oftn bi-in leik máner G anzd in spi G frö der in
uard sound tu der bredd seluz, & kontrariuciz
de

de-urds ending uiđ bređđ konsonants in sum
plas,me (uiđout ani-ofens tu đ'er) tak đe sound
ov đer áfein beginning đe next urd : or đe láter
ov đe first urd bi Ganǯed from sound tu bređ,
huen her soûded áfein begineţ đe foluing urd. ∞
/ and đe leik me hápn betuixt đe four uđer perǯ,
tu uit b, and p : ǫ, and k : ʒ, and G : d, and t,
and giv đe béter sound : huiG duţ beautifi
everi langaʒ. ∞ / it me bi aulso, đat ani on ov
đe sounded ov đe sevn perǯ, kómonlei in on urd,
at đ'end đer-of,me lev đe sound and bi obedient
tu đe bređ ov ani on ov đe sevn bređđ as fór
hav takn : teim me feind it gud tu sé haţ takn :
for feind faut, to se feint faut : and suG leik :
iet until ui spek so, ei kno no man uil ureit so ∞
/ but đis iʒ tu bi noted đat ani ov đe bređđ ov
đe sevn perǯ, most kó nonlei at đ'end ov đe fór-
mer urd,huer đe foluing begineţ uiđ on voël or
mor, iʒ Ganǯed intu her áfein sounded , and
đat bei đ'áfinite-it haţ uiţ đe voël,huiG ei hav
muG observed aʒ reʒon uaʒ ∞ / aulso huen on
voël endeţ on urd, and an-uđer begineţ đe foluing, ei hav iuʒd đe lein ov konʒunksion tu giv
knoleʒ đe me not bi ʒiuined in diphthong.∞
/ and iet đe ar sounded round tu-geđer , exept
huen aʒ đe first is steid de teim ov a kóma. ∞

and d'apostrophe ei hav iuzd tu tak a-ue a konso-
ıant az-uel az a voël, ıet but seldum.

/ but dez diferenses ui hav not foud in our fır-
mer maner ov ureiting nor neuer kould du. ∞
/ nor iet (az is sed) kan ani man bi serten huiG
t'iuz, and huiG tu lev, until it bi-uid a mor
studıı souht for, den hats bin iet atempted, huiG
ci trust summ man uil Sortli tak in hand, for de
uelts ov his kuntre. ∞/ and in de mean teim ci
present iu dıs, az a toʰn ov mei gud uil.

/ der iz aulso- a diskresıon in ureiting betuixt
a, mei, dei, fro, and no : and an, mein, dein,
from and non. ∞/ a, iz fıtlei-uritn huen
de-urd foluing beginets uid a konsonant, but
uid voël or dıiphthong de n, steits de gaping ov
de tu voëls huiG els Suldkum tugeder : de leik
ov de rest : and non iz aulso-in stid ov ne-on or
noᵗ on.∞/ so for tu-and til, huen de presıding
urd Saul end uid d, or t, un, dets kum fıtli betuixt de t, ov tu or til, and de former d,or t, tu
seperat an overmuG sound or breding ov dem :
so dat send untu-us, and hi sent untu-iu, iz
beter sed and so uritn, den send tu-us, or hi sent
tu-iu, for so spokn de muht giv okazion tu de
herer t'under-st,and, send us, and hi sent iu ∞
/in huiG and uder suG leik de diskresıon ov
de

de-ureiter uil-b:-iuꝛd ∾ / and for mei former
ſort ureiting, iu must konſider mei regard tu ꝺe
pronuſiaſion, huiꞬ ꝺe mulƚitiud ivn ov ꝺe beſt
ſpokn, du-iuꝛ aꝛ diꝛ urd kómaundment, der iꝛ
non but / ſpelerꝛ du ſe kómaundement huiꞬ iꝛ
ꝺe / frenꝺ ſound, and ureiting, ꝺe / duꞬ ma⅁
ſeꝛ ſilb f.r ſilabꝺ, / claꝛ, / hanꞩ, and / linke for
our / nꙇkles, / ꝫon, and / kꙇterin, ꝺe taking ſo
muꞬ ov ꝺe / latin as ꝺe froht gud, huo kan let
dem tu ureit aꝛ ꝺe ſpek, or us to ureit ours aꝛ
abuv, ſiing ui ſpek ſo. ∾ / ꝺe ſkótiꞩ ſpiꞬ iꝛ
tuil-iu, for our huat uil-iu, huei me ꝺe not
boldlei ureit it ſo? ∾ / nou for teꞬing tu riꝺ,
Quintilian ſeꞩ it iꝛ not gud tu teꞬ ꝺe
nams and order ov ꝺe léters, beſor ꝺe ꝼaps, huiꞬ
hi ſau mani du-in hiꝛ deꝛ, huerfor ꝺe tꞬer
ꝼuld Ꝼanꝛ and vari ꝺer order diverſlei, d⅁at ꝺe
lerner muht print in hiꝛ memori ꝺer ꝼaps, and
ſo bei ſiing dem tu bi-abꝺ tu nam dem : ivn aꝛ
ꝺe beſt ue tu kno a man, iꝛ bei ꝺe ſiht ov hiꝛ fa-
vour & proporſion, huer-bei his nam iꝛ ꝺe bétcr
retend. ∾ / furꝺer bi kómendeꞩ d'ius ov ſum
ov hiꝛ deꝛ : huiꞬ mad ꝺer léters ov / ivori, and
gav dem tu ꝺer Ꝼilder tu plꙇe : or huat-ſo-ever
as muht bi invenꝺed for ꝺe ſpidier plꙇſing and
preꝛerving ov ꝺe léters ꝼaps and nams, in ꝺe memori ov ꝺe riud, huoꝛ kounsel ci u.ld folo, if ei

Q. 3. did

did set furſ an / a, / b, / c, for ðe teſing oꝛ ðe
riud tu ꝛid, but uðeruei҃ ðen haſ bin iet dun.

/ nou ei uil end iuſ Quintilians uꝛds after hi had treated in his ſed firſt buk . 12 . Gap-
terꝝ firſt oꝛ ðe hop ðe ſaðer ſuld hav oꝛ ðe Gild
boꝛn, huat nurses, hut ſkulmasters and tutors,
and in huat ſpiſ and exersi҃ hi ſuld bi broht
up in. ∞ / at ð'end oꝛ his orthographi hi ſeſ tu
ðis éfekt foluing , ei kauł tu meind ðat ðer bi
sum uil ſink ðe҃ máterꝝ hu r-of ei hav uritn,
tu bi but treiſłꝝ, aud a hinderans tu him ðat
muht bi béter ókupied. ∞ / noꝛ ei ſink it mit
tu fiul into ð'extrem trubł, and fuʼlſ kavila-
lasions, ðerbei tu hurt and diminiſ mens uits:
but no part oꝛ / grámer huꝛteſ, but ðat huiſ i҃
superfluꝝ. ∞ / huat, ua҃ M. Tullius ð'orator
ani ſiŋg ðe les, foꝛ ðat hi ua҃ most dili҃ent in
in ði҃ art, and ðat hi kóꝛekted hi҃ sun҃ faultꝝ,
a҃ it ápird in hi҃ / epistłꝝ ? or did ðe bukꝝ huiſ
C. Cǽſar mad oꝛ / analo҃i brek his urðines ?
or ua҃ Meſſala nitidus ðe lés, bikau҃ hi mad
serten huol bukꝝ, not onli oꝛ evri-uꝛd, but aulso
oꝛ ðe léters. Non obſtant hæ diſciplinæ
per illas euntibus, ſed circa illas hæ-
rentibus. ∞ / huiſ signifeiéſ, ðe҃ instruksi-
ons hinder not suſ a҃ du pas bei ðem , but suſ
a҃ stikꝝ and ar (as it uer) tꝛid in ðem.

/ exampłꝝ

An Orthography.

/exampls hou serten uðer nasions du sound
ðer leters, boð in /latin, and in ðer mu-
ðer tung, ðerbei tu kno ðe beter hou
tu pronouns ðer spices, and
so tu rid ðem as ðe du.
/kap. viij.

or ðe konfirmasion ov ðat
huic̱ is sed, for ðe sounds az-
uel of voëls az of konsonants:
aulðoh ei hav in divers plases hier-befor seuëd iu, hou
serten uðer nasions du sound
part ov ðer leters : ei troht it gud hier, not onli
to rekapitulat and ʃortli rehers, part ov ðe befor mensioned, but aulso tu giv iu t'understand hou ðe du sound suc̱ ðer leters, az ð'ig-
norãt ðer-of ʃuld áproc̱ noting ner tu ðer pronunsiasion, beiriding ðer ureitings or prints ∞
/huerfor, huo so-iz dezeirous tu rid ð° /ita'ian
and ðe /latin as ðe du, hi must sound ðe voëlz
az ei hav súfisientli sed treating ov ðem, and az
ei hav iuzd ðem in aul dis niu maner, onli ex-
epting ðat ðe mak dis figiur u, konsonant az-
uel az dis v. ∞ /ðer c, ðe iuz after aul voëlz
as ui ðe k₂ (as ðer prozenitors ðe /latins ðid)
and

*The /italians do
writ u consonant
as u. bowill.*

after the vowl
iz R ... no ... in Itali-
... i ui as
... englilh. ch.
... R.

... i ui
as ... englilh
... conant.
for it ícher
a o u. ...

and iuz not k, at aul: but dᶔe-abiuz dᶔe c, bifor e, and i, in dᶔe sound ov our ch, or G, az ecce and accioche, dᶔe sound ekGe, akGioke, trancef- co, franGesko, fece, facendo, amici, feGe fazendo, amiGi: and for dᶔe sound ov de k, dᶔe iuz ch.∞/ dᶔer g, dᶔe kip az ei hav dun after voelz, and befor a, o, and u: but befor e, and i, dᶔe hav abiuzd it uidus, for huiG ei hav iuzd z, and tu kip dat sound befor a, o, and u, dᶔe u- zurp gi, as hath bin sed, and dᶔerfor dᶔe never mak dᶔe i, konsonant, for dᶔe se not aginto, but aiuto, az we bi dus ai-uto.∞/ dᶔe t, dᶔe never sound in s, iz in protettion, satisfattion, dᶔe sound de t, hard, and dᶔerfor dubld-it in doz urds and man- i-udᶔers: but in /giurifditioni, /militia, /sententia, /intentione, and mani-udᶔers dᶔe du not dubl it, iet dᶔe sound it as it iz, and ne- ver turn it intu dᶔe sound ov s, but iv iu markit uel, dᶔe breᶿ ov dᶔe t, pasing trub dᶔe tiᶠ, and turning tu de-i, duᶠ mak it sim as it uer ner dᶔe sound ov de,s, but iz not dᶔerfor so in efekt.∞ /for dᶔer gh, dᶔe du not sound g, so hard az ui uld, but so softli az it iz oftn uritn and printed uidout dᶔe g.∞/ dᶔer zz, dᶔe sound most komo- li dᶔe first z, in t, as in /fortezza, /grandezza, /deftrezza, but at sum teims dᶔe sound dem

gli.

zz as R.

az

az de du cc, as for diz nam de-ureit indiferentli
Eccellino, or Ezzellino. ∞ / de hav aulso de
sound ov our ſh or ſ, huiĉ de-ureit ſc, befor, e,   sce · sci · hi, hi
or i: de-inz tu-ureit de th, but not for our th, or
ħ: for de hav not de soūd ſcrofin aul der ſpiĝ,
nor ov d, & sound it in / matthio, az me bi mat-
hio, as of th, iz sed in / thomas and / thames. ∞
/ and for lak ov a knolez for de ku entiti̥z ov der
voël̥z de-ar konstrend tu dubĺ der konsonant̥s
oftn and muĝ : and for de longer teim ov der
voël̥s, de hav no mark: huerfor huo so-iz dezei-
ruz tu rid der ureiting uel, and imitat der pronunsiasion had nid tu hav sum instruksion bei
de leivli vois. ∞ / and huen de du rez der tiun
ov der urds (huiĉ iz oftn) de not it uid de / latin gravtiun, d'us, andò, parlò, e moſtrò
la nouità, al podeſtà de la città. ∞
/ and in riding de / latin, aul dat de feind
writn, de du pronouns, ivn as de du der mu-
der tung, in de veri sounds befor-sed.

/ for de hih duĝ de sound aul der voël̥z in   Hiǵh Dutche.
de veri sam sort: and never mak de i, konsonant,   j
nor abiuz de g, befor de c, and i, az d' / ita-   g
lian duħ, but kip it auluez befor dem, az befor
a, o, and u: & de / ſleming tu bi siur tu kontiniu
dat sound, dud iuz it befor e, and i, uid, h. ∞   gh·

R.I.   / nor

/ nor haƒ de / duG (over nor neder) dat sound
huiG iz de leik ov our j, konsonant, and d'italian gi, befor-sed, for huiG ci iuz z, but de bref

tsch. der-of de hih / duG haƿ, er ureit it uid tsch. ∞

/ and bod de figiurs for de firƒ voël, de iuz
uidout ani serten diferens huiG Suld bi voël
or huiG konsonant : and den haƿ de de diphthongs befor namd, / folio.zr.pa.z. huiG ar tu bi
noted ov dat / ingliS man huiG Saul dezeir
tu lern der tung. ∞ / and du-iuz tu dubd der
voelz for der longer teim. ∞ / de haƿ aulso

sch. our sound ov ſh, or S, for huiG de iuz ſch, as
ſcham, ſchale, ſleiſch and fiſch, de soûd as ui me
Sci. sce. Sam, Sel, fleS, fiS, and ſce, ſci, de sound az duƒ
aulso d' / italian : and az ui du Se, Si. ∞ / de
never put de c, intu de sound of s, but iuz
k, tu bi-out of dout. ∞ / de iuz de Q, veri
seldum, but de k, muG in plas der-of, and
de-a, de du-oftn sound broder den ui du, but
muG aulso-as ui du. ∞ / and for de rest de
pronouns aul de-ureit, and kip der leters in
de self sound, huer-in de rid aulso der
/ latin. ∞

Spanish.
3 e z. — / nou ſirdli for de / spaniard hi abiuzeth
de i, and u, in konsonants as ui-and de / frenS
du, and de u, oftn, in de / frenS and / skótiS

tiſ sound : and ƌe *ch,* in / *muchacho* aʒ ui du ch .
in Ɠalk and Ɠiʒ : but for aul ƌer uƌer voëʒ
and léters, ƌe iuʒ dem in ƌe sam sounds ƌat du
ƌ° / *italian* and / *duƓ,* but ƌat ƌę iuʒ ƌe *y,* y.
aʒ ui haʋ dun (buiƓ neƌer / *italian* nor / *dauƓ*
niƌ) tu bi ƌerbei eʒd oʋ ƌe dout oʋ ƌe *i,* konsonant huiƓ ƌe sound leik ƌe / frenſ. ∞ / ƌe *c,*
ƌe iuʒ in s, uiƌout ani noʇ oʋ diſcrens befor *e,* c .
and *i.* but befor *a, o,* and *u,* ƌę haʋ deueiʒd
a-litƌ, s, under ƌus, *ç: de-iuʒ* nʋer ƌe *k,* but ƌe ç
Q, uiſi ƌ° / *italian* : ƌe-iuʒ ƌe *ll,* in ƌe sound oʋ ll .
ƌ, uiƌ ƌe ualſ. ∞ / ƌe *u,* in *quæ* and, qui, qu.
ƌe du seldum sound, as for *que quieres,* ƌę
sound as ui mę ke *kierez.* ∞ / and for aul ƌe rest
ƌe kip ƌe aunsient / *latin* sound, and so riƌ
ƌer / *latin* aʒ du ƌ° / *italian* and / zermain :
and for him ƌat haſi ƌe / *latin* tung uiƌ a-litƌ
instruksion iʒ aʒ eʒi tu riƌ and under-stand
aʒ iʒ ƌ° / *italian.* ∞

/ and nou last oʋ aul, ƌe / frenſ, uiƌ ƌ° a- *French. alphab*
bius oʋ ƌe *u,* in ƌe skótiſ leik sound. oʋ ƌe in *v*.
diphthong, huiƓ, nor / *italian,* nor / *duƓ* did
ever giʋ tu *u:* and iuʒing ƌe *g,* and *j,* konsonant *g. ε j.*
in ƌe sound huer-of, our ſ, iʒ ƌe breƌed konso-
nant : and turning ƌe *s,* intu ʒ, huen ui, uiƌ aul s
ƌe rest, du sound ƌe *s,* (exept ƌe / *spaniard,* aʒ

An Orthography.

ui hav aulso iuʒd betuixt tu voelʒ) and kiping
an uſer teim in ðer voëlʒ ðen ui du, and iuʒing
o e ðer e, in ðeivers sounds, and ðe o, ſumhuat aul-
qu so : bei not sounding ðe u , in qui, and quæ,
but aʒ ui me ki, and ke, uid leving mani ov ðer
leters vnsounded, duʒ kauʒ ðer spiG veri hard
tu bi lernd bei art , & not eʒi bei ðe leivli vois,
aʒ it iʒ notoriuʒli knon . ∞ / so aʒ if ei Suld
ureit / frenS, in ðe leters and order huiG ei du
nou-iuʒ, ei-am serten ðat iu Suld muG suner
kum tu ðer pronunsiasion, ðer-bei , ðen bei
ureiting aʒ ðe du. ∞ / and tu experiment ðe
mater, and tu mak suG aʒ understand / frenS,
juʒes ðer-of, ei uil ureit ðe / lords prer aʒ ðe
du, huiG Suld be preʒēted tu suG an on, aʒ kan
rid ðis maner , and ict understandi ti not ðe
/ frenS, and peuv hou hi kan rid and pronouns
it : and ðen present it him in ðis maner ov ureiting, aʒ hier-after : and kompar his pronunsiasion tu ðe former, and iu Suld puv ðat efekt,
huiG kan not bi broht tu pás bei our form.r maner . ∞ / and ðer-for hier soluefs ðe / lords prer
first in / frenS in ðer maner ov ureiting. Noſtre pere qui es és cieux, Ton nom ſoit
ſanctifié. Ton Regne aduienne. Ta vo-
lonte ſoit faite en la terre comme au
ciel.

ciel.Donne-nous au-iourd'huy noſtre
pain quotidian:Et nous pardonne nos
offenſes, comme nous pardonnons à
ceux qui nous ont offensez . Et ne
nous indui point en tentation : mais
nous deliure du mal. <u>Gar à toy</u> eſt le
regne,la puiſſance , & la gloire és ſiecles, des ſiecles. Amen. ∞/*nou in d'is niu*
maner az foluëts. ∞ /*notrah perah ki-ez ez sieuz,*
tun /*num soit saniifié.* ∞ /*tun* /*rénah avié-*
nah. ∞/*ta volumté soit fétah, an la tárah ku-*
mah o siel . Dúne-nuz o zzurdui notrah pen
kotidian . Enu pardunah noz óſanses kúmah
nu pardúnunz a scuz ki nuz unt óſansez . / e ne
nuz indui point an tantasion : mez nu delivrah
diu mad.∞/*kar a toe et le renah, la piuisánse*
e la gloerah ez siekles dez siekles /aman.∞ /*nou*
kontrariuuiz uil ei ureit hier-under in dez niu
léters (and kiping der sound az beſor) hou de
/frenG du pronouns der /latin: and d'at aul-
so in de /lords prer, huG iz az d'us. ∞/ *pater*
noster kiez in seliz,santifisctiur nomen tiuium,
at veniat reinium tiuium fiat voluntaz tiuá
sikiut in selo e in táva panem nostrinm kotidi-
anium da nobiz odie & dimite nobi debita
nostra, sikiut et noz dimitimiuz debitoribiuz
R.3. *nostriz.*

c nostriz ∞/et ne noz indiukaz in tentasionem :
/set libera noz a malo. ∞/ and ei remember or
a meri zest ei hav herd or a bue huiG did heip a
/frenſ pri t at más, huo seing dominiu vobi-
kium, de bue hering it sound stranʒli-in hiz er,
aunsuered, eti kum tirleri tikium, and so uent
laubing his ue ∞/ and so peradventiur iu-uil
at deriding, aʒ iu me biliv me-ei did at de
ureiting hier-of. ∞/ ei kald ureit aulso hou de
frenſ and uder forens du spek /ingliſ, but der
maner is so plentiful in mani-of our erz, aʒ ei
tink it superfliuz.∞/ de rezen huei de kan not
sound our spiG, iz (aʒ iu me persev bei dat is
sed) bikauz ui hav and iuz serten sounds and
bredz huiG de hav not, and du-aulso iuʒ tu
sounds sum ov doz leters huiG de-iuʒ uid us, u-
deruerʒ den de du: and de for revenʒ sum ov
ourz userueriʒ den ui du. huiG iz de kauz aulso
dat der spiGes ar hard for us tu rid, but de
soud ons knon, ui kan ezili pronouns ders bei de
rezon abuvsed. ∞/ and dus tu-end if iu tink
litd profit tu bi in dis huer-in ei hav kaused iu
tu pás ur teim, ei uil iet disGarʒ mei self dat
ei-am dsiured it kan du-iu no harm, and so de
aulmihti/god, giver ov aul gud tings, blis uz
aul, and send us his grás in dis transitori leif,

and

and in de uorld tu kum, leif everlasting. ∞
/ so bi-it. ∞

FINIS.

Sat cito ſi ſat bene.

/ an aduertiȝment touᴖing d'order
ov de foluing tabł.

/ bikauȝ de voëls and konsonants ar devci-
ded intu suᴖ parts aȝ befor, dis tabł duth
kip dem in de leik order : tu-uit first a, e, i,
o, u, and den de four perȝ huiᴖ ar mad uid
a stóping breth : tu uit b, p : d, t : g, k : and j,
ᴖ.∞ / den d'uder thri thrulei bredd peys, tu
uit d, th : v, f : and ȝ, s .∞ / den de. 5. semi-
uokals l, m, n, r, and ł, and de tu breds ᵹ, and
h: aulso, for dat in d'order befor iuȝd, deȝ niu
leters ar not komprehended. ∞ / huer-for dis
tabł is plaſed and set in suᴖ order as foluëth.

R. 4. / s

A Table.

A Table

A Table

A Table

A Table

                                            of

A Table

S.3.   /kon-

A Table

óka-

A Table

S.4.   / vois

A Table

/v

/ vois simpɬ iʒ d'element ov de spiꞬ and de
leter ov ureiting.   fol 9.pɑ.1

/ vises in ⎰ / diminusion.   fol.14 pa.2
our ureit- ⎱ / superfluite. from fol.15.tu. 21.
ting.4.   / uʒurpasion.   fol 21
             / misplasing.   fol. 21.22.pa.1

/ voels hou de bi maɖ uiɬ d'instruments ov de
    mouϑ.   fol.30

/ v, kept aul-uai ꞃonsonant bei de / briuts. fo.31

/ voëls der aunsient, ʒuꞇt and diu souuds pruvd
    bei deivers stranʒ langaʒes , and aulso bei
    / ingliꟅ.   fol.33.34

/ſ

/ first inventers of leters unserten .   fol.8.pa 2

/ ſ, taꞁn amongst de / latins for d'aspirasion, b.
                                            fol.50.pa.1

/ ſ, iuʒd bei de / latins uder-ueiʒ den did de
    / griks Φ.   fol.50

de / frenꞬ sound ov der leterʒ.   fol.65.66.pɑ.1

de / frenꟅ, hou de pronuns der / latin.   fol.66

/ʒ

/ʒ, and s, huen d'on or d'uder me bi most kon-
    venientli-uritn.   fol.60.pɑ.2
                                              / spiꞬ

A Table

A Table

A Table

T.z.   H,

A Table

FINIS.

Seene and allowed according to the
order appointed.

¶ Imprinted at London,
by William Seres, dwelling
at the west ende of Paules, at
the signe of the Hedge-
hog, &c.